Flashes in Her Soul

THE HIDDEN VOICES SERIES

Flashes in Her Soul: The Life of Jabu Ndlovu

Jean Fairbairn
with a new Introduction by Debby Bonnin

HIDDEN VOICES

Second edition published by Fanele, an imprint of
Jacana Media (Pty) Ltd, in 2018

10 Orange Street
Sunnyside
Auckland Park 2092
South Africa
+2711 628 3200
www.jacana.co.za

First edition published by Buchu Books 1991
Original text © Jean Fairbairn, 1991
New introduction © Debby Bonnin, 2018

All rights reserved.

ISBN 978-1-928232-52-0

Cover design by Shawn Paikin
Set in Stempel Garamond 10.5/14pt
Printed and bound by Shumani Mills Communications,
Parow, Cape Town
Job no. 003174

See a complete list of Jacana titles at www.jacana.co.za

 HIDDEN VOICES

The financial assistance of the National Institute of the Humanities and Social Sciences (NIHSS) towards this research is hereby acknowledged. Opinions expressed and conclusions arrived at are those of the authors and editors and are not necessarily to be attributed to the NIHSS.

As I climbed up the mountain I expected to see houses ...
But I saw ashes
I looked up at the sky to ask Heavens
About the talented and gifted people of P.M.Burg

Where is Khopho? I asked
A woman with a mountain voice
A woman with silky golden voice
There was no response from Heavens

Where is Jabu?
A woman with flashes in her soul
A woman with fires in her heart
A woman with lion strength
Again there was no response from the sky

Extract from "Pietermaritzburg" by Makhosi Khoza

Contents

Foreword ix
Acknowledgements xii
Maps xiv

Introduction to the second edition, by Debby Bonnin ... 1

Introduction to the first edition 35
1   A gifted child 41
2   Imbali 55
3   A very harmonious home 63
4   MAWU comes to Prestige 69
5   We want to join! 74
6   I used to be just a quiet person 78
7   Comrade and friend 82
8   The year the war began 89
9   The Sarmcol strike 95
10 We are crying in Maritzburg 100
11 There is no peace 110

12 Sisters of the Long March 112
13 Defending Stage I 117
14 The attack 121
15 Calls for peace 127
16 Linda 132
17 Warlords stand trial 137
18 Conclusion: The trust 140

Index 149

Foreword

THE HIDDEN VOICES PROJECT EMERGED out of an interest in left intellectual contributions towards discussions on race, class, ethnicity and nationalism in South Africa. Specifically, the project seeks to examine and make available writings by Hidden Voices – voices outside of the university system, or academic voices suppressed by apartheid pressures. Before and during the apartheid years, many universities were closed to existing local ideas and debates, and critical intellectual debates, ideas, texts, poetry and songs often originated outside academia during the period of the struggle for liberation.

The Hidden Voices Series seeks to publish key texts, books, documents and other materials that were never published under apartheid, or seminal books that have gone out of print. We hope that these recovered, lost or forgotten voices will help to reinvigorate the humanities and social sciences, and contribute to the decolonisation of knowledge production in South Africa, and indeed throughout Africa.

Jabu Ndlovu was assassinated in May 1989. This second volume in the Hidden Voices Series – *Flashes in Her Soul: The Life of Jabu Ndlovu*, by Jean Fairbairn – is a reprint of a 1991 publication produced by the Natal Worker History Project and the National Union of Metalworkers of South Africa in an effort to provide support for the Ndlovu family's surviving children. It focuses on the life and times of Jabu Ndlovu, a strong woman – wife, mother, worker, union activist – who fought for the rights of her fellow workers and community members. She lived at a particularly difficult time in apartheid South Africa, and her story is representative of the lives of many women living and working in those turbulent times.

Flashes in Her Soul is republished with a new introduction by Debby Bonnin, Associate Professor and Head of the Sociology Department at the University of Pretoria. She was actively researching and writing during the years that this book describes. Her introduction addresses several key dynamics that affected people's lives in KwaZulu-Natal at that time:

1. spatial issues arising from colonisation and apartheid, including the dispossession of African people from their land and the resulting move to towns and cities;
2. the proletarianisation of African people and their entry into a labour force defined by race and gender;
3. the re-emergence of the trade union movement in South Africa; and
4. the violence and civil war in KwaZulu-Natal that cost many people, including Jabu, their lives.

This book, and indeed the entire series, has been made possible by the generous support of the National Institute for the Humanities and Social Sciences (NIHSS). The Institute was established in December 2013 to advance and coordinate scholarship, research and ethical practice in the field of humanities and the social sciences (HSS). Its catalytic projects aim to encourage research in new areas of engaged HSS scholarship.

We would like to thank Jean Fairbairn for giving her permission to republish this book. We also thank the surviving children of Jabu and Jabulani Ndlovu – her daughter Luhle and her son Sanele – for endorsing the republication of this book.

Karin Pampallis and Edward Webster
Hidden Voices Project
Johannesburg, October 2017

Acknowledgements

These are the acknowledgements and thanks as they appeared in the first edition in 1991.

With thanks to the following:
- Jabu's family, especially her mother, her sisters and her children for the time they spent working with us on the book.
- Jabu's comrades, colleagues and friends for granting us interviews. They are the many people referred to as "a comrade" or "a friend" in the text. Although they had much to say, they did not want to be named because they feared for their lives.
- The National Union of Metalworkers of South Africa, especially the Pietermaritzburg Local, for assisting with our research.
- John Aitchison of the Centre for Adult Education of the University of Natal, Pietermaritzburg, whose research deepened our understanding of the war.
- Jabu Ndlovu and Thulani Mshengu of the Natal Worker History Project for their help and translation.

- Astrid von Kotze and others at the University of Natal, including members of the Natal Worker History Project Steering Committee, for their help with design, editing and proofreading.
- The BTR Workers' Support Network in the UK for their assistance with distribution abroad and publication of the Zulu text, including the following: NALGO – Cambridge City Branch, Manchester Area Health Services Branch, Leicester Branch; MSF – Eastern Region, Cambridge General Branch; NGA – Mid Anglia Branch; Cambridge and District Co-operative Society; Cambridge Trades Council; Huntingdon and St Neots Trades Council; Grapevine Bookshop; and all the other organisations and individuals who donated to the Jabu Ndlovu Family Appeal Fund.
- The Labor Video Project based in San Francisco, California, for letting us use transcripts of an interview they did with Jabu, and Maureen Anderson of the BTR Workers' Support Network for transcribing the interview.
- Pictures by:[1]
  - Jean Fairbairn, pages 1, 16
  - Afrapix, pages pages 36
  - Aron Mazel, pages 19, 57, 62, 76
- The Natal Worker History Project is funded by the Southern African Catholic Bishops' Conference Church and Work Commission.

---

[1] Update, October 2017: Only some of the photographs that appeared in the first edition were available for use in this edition. Photo credits for second edition: Aron Mazel – cover, p 105, p 128; Jean Fairbairn – p 44, p 64; Ndlovu family – p 50.

Maps

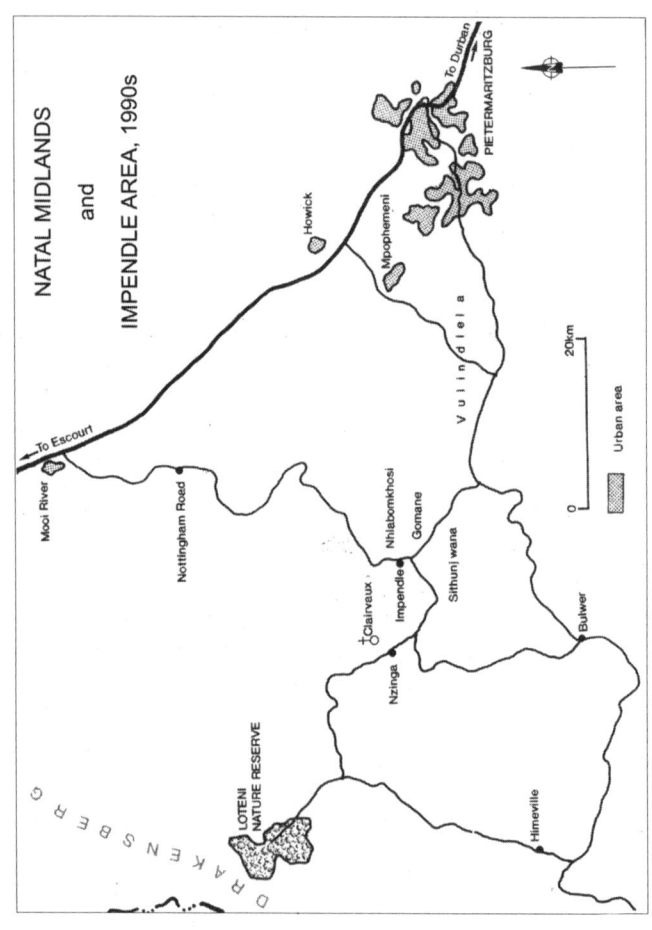

Flashes in Her Soul

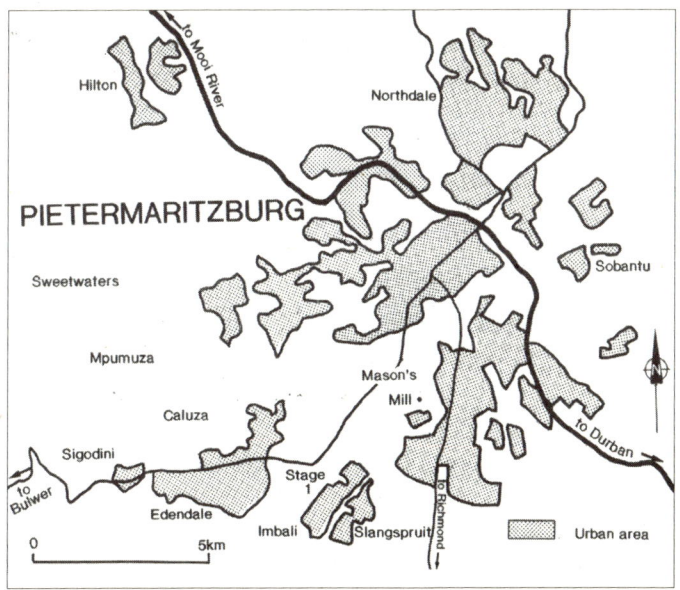

Introduction to the second edition

by Debby Bonnin

RUNNING DOWN THE CENTRE of Pietermaritzburg is Jabu Ndlovu Street. Who, you might ask, is this Jabu Ndlovu that she has a street named after her? This book tells the story of Jabu's life – the life of an ordinary woman growing up during the height of apartheid. But while she might have been an ordinary woman, apartheid was not an ordinary time. As Jabu's story shows, it forced ordinary people to do extraordinary deeds and to pay the price for their tenacity and bravery.

This book details Jabu's life, her struggles and her achievements. Her life story mirrors the lives of many African women in KwaZulu-Natal during the apartheid era. The trajectories of history that buffeted Jabu and her family are the same as those which shaped the opportunities and working lives of many of the African people of KwaZulu-Natal. Her family, like other African families, faced the multiple pressures brought about by the colonial conquest of Natal, the development of a capitalist economy in the region and the enactment of numerous apartheid laws. All this squeezed their access to land, eventually forcing them to move from the countryside to the cities. In the city, many of these women became factory workers. As they became aware of the way in which they were exploited and oppressed as black workers, they joined trade unions and, in some cases, like Jabu, rose to leadership positions within the union movement. When political violence engulfed the province, Jabu stood tall against it. She spoke out, she supported the youth, and she refused to bow down. As a result, she and her family were targeted. Jabu, like many other women, lost her life in that violence.

Jabu's life cuts across four significant dynamics in KwaZulu-Natal's history during the twentieth century. First, there is the history of how African families came to live where they do now; related to this is the history of dispossession of the land during the periods of colonisation and apartheid. Second, and closely linked to the struggles over land, are the ways in which Africans were proletarianised and entered a labour market shaped by race and gender stratification. Third is the rise of the independent trade union movement, including the way in which ordinary workers rose to leadership positions and shaped that movement. It was their struggles that created a new workplace and helped to topple the apartheid regime. And lastly, there is the civil war that divided families and neighbourhoods and ultimately cost Jabu her life. Each of these four areas is discussed below.

Colonialism and conquest

Following their defeat of the Zulu King Dingane at the Battle of Ncome, the Voortrekkers claimed the area south of the Thukela River and north of the Mzimkhulu River, and declared the Republic of Natalia in 1938 (Slater, 1980: 150). The Voortrekker Republic set up its capital in Pietermaritzburg, naming it after two Boer leaders. Many of these settlers saw Natal as an empty land available to be occupied by them. The trekkers registered land claims on this land, but much of it remained unoccupied by them.

However, Natal was not "empty". As a result of the conflict associated with the establishment of the Zulu kingdom by Shaka and later Dingane, many people living south of the Thukela River had fled their ancestral lands to seek refuge in the veld and forests. However, from the 1830s they began to return to their historical lands (Guy, 2013: 26). The Boer Volksraad did not have either the military or the administrative capacity to evict these African households. Concerned about the stability of the region, the British moved to occupy Port Natal (Morrell, Wright & Meintjes, 1996: 34). In 1843 they annexed Natal, signing an agreement with the trekker farmers that they would not interfere with their land tenure (Christopher, 1968).[2] However, within a few years most of the Boer settlers

---

[2] In 1842, a small British force was sent (by sea) from the Cape Colony to occupy Port Natal. The Boers resisted but were ultimately defeated by the British and the land between the Thukela River and Mzimkhulu River was formally annexed and became a British colony. The British signed an agreement with the Boers that allowed them to keep the land they claimed after defeating the Zulus. Christopher (1968) has argued that this agreement put in place the patterns of land ownership and settlement that have influenced land ownership to the present day.

had returned over the Drakensberg, and much of the land passed into the hands of land speculators (Slater, 1980). At this time there were between 50 000 and 100 000 Africans living between the Thukela and Mzimkhulu rivers, some in well-established chiefdoms that had managed to survive the upheavals of the conflict in the region and others in smaller dispersed groups (Morrell et al, 1996: 35). In contrast, there were only 6 000 British settlers (Morrell et al, 1996: 35).

For much of the early nineteenth century, the African homestead economy successfully re-established itself alongside attempts by the settlers to establish commodity production. African communities supplied maize, vegetables and wood to the colonial towns of Durban and Pietermaritzburg (Slater, 1980: 156). The surplus produced by the homestead economy supported the colonial state (Lambert, cited in Morrell et al, 1996: 38). The colonial authorities tried unsuccessfully to establish commercial agriculture in the region, assisting the settlers in many ways (Slater, 1980: 153; Morrell et al, 1996: 34–7). Throughout the century, the settler farmers put pressure on the colonial authorities to remove land from Africans and to force Africans to enter wage labour. The settler farmers saw the success of African agriculture as an obstacle to their own success (Slater, 1980: 158).

In the late 1840s, Theophilus Shepstone, Secretary for Native Affairs in the Colony of Natal, began the process of creating the reserve system with the establishment of eight African locations (Guy, 2013: 112–14). The land allocated was a small part of the total area of the Colony, and was insufficient to accommodate the Colony's African population. Furthermore, only a small portion of the African population lived in these reserves; many lived outside of them as labourers, tenants or squatters on Crown or private land (Morrell et al, 1996: 36). In many instances these lands were devoid of settler occupation and, for those living there, their occupation was undisturbed by the settlers. Yet, over the course of the nineteenth century, this situation changed. As more settlers arrived in the Colony, they enforced the "Colonial laws to assert their rights over land and labour" (Morrell et al, 1996: 36); they frequently called for the reserves to be broken up, believing that this would force African people into wage labour. These pressures were resisted by the colonial government and in 1864 Shepstone succeeded in placing the African reserves under the administration of the Natal Native Trust (later the South African Native Trust, SANT), a government body that safeguarded African rights to hold communal title to their land. By this stage, there were a total of 42 reserves in Natal totalling 836 509 hectares, but much of this land "was of inferior quality – generally very hilly and agriculturally less viable than the lands retained for the white colonists" (SPP, 1983: 18, 19).

The "Shepstone system", as the reserves became known, was one of indirect rule that would allow the colonial government to rule African people through the agency of African chiefs. While some of these *amakhosi* had a hereditary claim to rule their people, others were appointed to replace those who incurred the wrath of the colonial powers (Guy, 2013). All Africans living in the Colony, whether or not they lived in a reserve, were ultimately placed under a chief and required to *ukukhonza*.[3] Over

---

[3] The verb *khonza* means "to submit to" or "to pay respect to". To *ukukhonza iNkosi* means "to pay homage to, show respect to or give allegiance to the chief".

the course of the nineteenth century, a system of African "customary law" was codified using a mixture of indigenous custom and British law. The Natal Code of Native Law was passed by the Natal Legislative Council in 1891. According to the Natal Code, women were subjugated to men and children to their father; legally, women became permanent minors. Guy (1997) has called the Shepstone system an "accommodation of the patriarchs" because it enforced patriarchal and gerontocratic power.

Outside of the reserve areas, other families "squatted" on unalienated Crown lands[4] or unoccupied purchased land, though eventually these households were forced to pay rent. Others entered into labour relationships with white settler farmers; of these, Slater (1980: 160) indicates that stock farms were preferred as the work was not particularly difficult and there were opportunities for households to accumulate cattle. The least desirable work was labour service on a white commercial farm with its demanding conditions of labour tenancy – that is, free labour in exchange for access to land for grazing and subsistence.

The measures adopted by the colonial state to force African households to enter the cash economy intensified during the nineteenth century, often in response to demands of commercial farmers. They included taxes, tariffs on African-purchased imports, enforcement of European-style dress, fines and medical fees (Slater, 1980: 161). The alternative to labour tenancy on a white farm was to migrate to the cities or the mines in search of waged

---

[4] "Unalienated" land refers to land that was "unallocated"; it was not held under lease or allocated for any other purpose. It automatically belonged to the Crown, and after 1910 to the state.

employment. However, for those colonial settlers who had taken occupation of land in the hope of becoming successful commercial farmers this situation was far from satisfactory. The settler farmers were in constant battle to secure labour for themselves, and persistently urged for the enforcement of the laws against squatting and for the white occupation of "unoccupied" land.

The purchase of land by Africans, either through mission schemes – as in Inanda (outside Durban), Edendale (outside Pietermaritzburg) or Georgedale and Woody Glen (in the Hammarsdale area) – or through individual tenure was one way to enable African ownership of land and to avoid proletarianisation. The first mission reserves were established in 1856, and by 1864 there were twenty-one (later adjusted to nineteen) (Bonnin, 2007: 89). Just as the settlers resisted the establishment of the reserves, so they resisted the Christian mission ideology of individual land tenure for Africans. Soon after achieving responsible government in 1883, the settlers implemented measures to restrict African access to land tenure (SPP, 1983: 25). In the 1890s, individual ownership within the mission reserves was no longer permitted, and in 1903 with the passing of the Mission Reserves Act, the Land Department was instructed to decline all African bids on the sale of crown land. The largest areas of African freehold land were to be found in the counties of Pietermaritzburg and Klip River. In the former, much of it was along the upper uMkhomazi river valley which ran through Impendle (SPP, 1983: 25). There were extensive purchases of land by Africans in the late nineteenth and early twentieth centuries, until halted by the 1913 Land Act.

Colonial conquest of the land and its people did not

happen peacefully. This was a time of violence, turmoil and increasing domination of the African people by the colonial authorities. Relationships between colonial authorities and some *amakhosi* that might have seemed to offer advantages were in time subjected to the will of the colonists, often under pressure from the settler farmers. One example is the "rebellion" of Langalibalele, the *iNkosi* of the Hlubi people, and the subsequent smashing of the Hlubi chiefdom. The survivors were brutally dispersed across the Colony, and the colonial authorities manufactured new "tribes" and imposed new *amakhosi* (Morrell et al, 1996: 48–9; Guy, 2013: 388–99). Also at this time, attitudes of white supremacy and racism developed among the settlers, eventually finding their way into oppressive and violent laws against African people (Lambert & Morrell, 1996: 68, 71; Guy, 2013). Between 1893 and 1910, at least 48 laws affecting Africans reached the statute books (Lambert & Morrell, 1996: 69).

The movement of people to the reserves was not willingly undertaken, and involved "cajoling or forcing into [the reserves] as many Africans as possible" (Morrell et al, 1996: 36). Besides open rebellion there were many incidents of passive resistance: for example, non-cooperation with colonial officials and the cutting of fences. Those evicted from their lands were accused of stealing, setting fires and stabbing cattle (Lambert & Morrell, 1996: 85). What particularly evoked the ire of African people was taxation, specifically the poll taxes imposed in 1905 (Marks, 1970; Guy, 2006). Although the Zondi people from the Umvoti district, under *iNkosi* Bhambatha kaMancinza, began the rebellion, the reprisals from the colonists following the defeat of the rebels were widespread.⁵ The homestead economy in these regions was laid to waste; fields and huts were burned and stock reduced. Facing prosecution and desperate poverty, the young men who had been the mainstay of the rebellion migrated in greater numbers than before to the gold mines of Johannesburg and the emerging industrial centre of Durban (Carton, 2000).

Jabu's father's family, the Mkhizes, came to settle in the area of Nhlabamkhosi at Impendle soon after her father, Phambano, was born in 1911. At the time, Impendle, in the foothills of the Drakensberg, was a small traditional authority area interspersed among white farmland, wattle plantations and freehold African land. The area fell under the chieftainship of Nxamalala. The Zondi and their various lineages, which included the Nxamalala or Zuma, had long held sway in the hills to the west and north of Pietermaritzburg (Guy, 2013: 86). Baba Lawrence Zondi from Gezubuso, a BTR Sarmcol worker and long-time trade unionist, indicated that many Zondi had moved to this area in the aftermath of the Bhambatha Rebellion. Households from the Mkhize clan had lived in the Upper uMkhomazi valley for decades, sometimes coming into conflict with the Zondi as the pressures over access to land increased (Guy, 2013: 304). The *iNkosi* allocated land to the family, and Jabu's grandfather set about building his house; they also had fields and were able to plant crops and keep cattle. Jabu's grandfather was a policeman in Impendle.

---

5   Open rebellion against the poll tax was initiated by the Zondi people but they were joined by young men from many parts of the Colony who both resented the tax and felt that the elders had given in to the demands of the British and betrayed the youth. Because of the widespread participation, the reprisals following the defeat of the rebels were also widespread and went beyond the lands of the Zondi.

In 1894 the Colony was granted responsible government. This strengthened the hand of commercial farmers, and a number of laws were passed to force Africans off the land and into wage labour (Lambert & Morrell, 1996). In 1910 the Colony of Natal became part of the Union of South Africa. Soon after that, the 1913 Land Act was passed. At first it had little impact in Natal, but in 1916 the Beaumont Commission, as the Natives Land Commission was known, made additional recommendations, and in the years that followed the amount of land available for African occupation decreased. The 1936 Native Trust and Land Act identified freehold areas that were to be added to the existing reserves; among these were the many freehold farms in the Impendle district (SPP, 1983: 35).

Land alienation and migration to the cities

By the time Jabu's father was 15, his father had died and he had to migrate to Durban in search of work. At that time, in 1926, Durban's industrialisation was limited and the major demand was for casual labour at the docks and during the holiday season (Maylam, 1996: 102). Even then, casual migrant work in Durban was a preferred option to farm work. According to Maylam (1996: 102), over 50% of the total African population in Durban in the mid-1920s were casual workers. Manufacturing development in Durban only accelerated after World War II. The other major city in the province was Pietermaritzburg, but it had little industrial development until the 1950s.

In the book Jabu's mother explains that she was working on white-owned farms in the Loteni area, not far from Impendle, when she met Jabu's father. Like many migrants at the time, Phambano moved between the city and the countryside, looking for work where he could find it, trying to avoid farm labour. They married in 1939, on the eve of World War II, and Phambano took his new wife to live in the family homestead at Impendle. Within a few years, Phambano had asked *iNkosi* Mconjwana Zuma for land. On this land he built a house for his family, planted fruit trees, grew crops and built a kraal for his cattle. Phambano was able to support his growing family from the land.

As in the nineteenth century, white commercial farmers were dissatisfied. They continued to complain about labour shortages. Throughout the 1940s the Natal Agricultural Union lobbied for more favourable conditions including "a proper system of registration and control of movement and employment" (Bonnin, 1987: 64). The National Party victory in the 1948 elections gave support to their cause, and in the next decade a range of legislation was passed. This included the Natives (Abolition of Passes) and Coordination of Documents Act (1952) and the Amendment of the Native Trust and Land Act (1956) which moved to regulate labour tenancy by providing for the registration of all labour tenant contracts (Bonnin, 1987: 64–5). Farmers were also unhappy with the activities of the South African Native Trust and pressed for the removal of "non-released African freehold farms" – that is, so-called black spots (SPP, 1983: 39). By the 1960s, as the apartheid state rolled out its spatial plan of racial division, the focus of the SANT moved to finding land to facilitate the relocation of labour tenants and black spots.

Evictions and relocations happened for a number of

different reasons – clearing of black spots, eviction of labour tenants, homeland consolidation, group areas, relocation of townships, removal of informal settlements, betterment planning,[6] and infrastructure development. Nevertheless, behind all these reasons lay the desire to separate the "races" and to control the supply and movement of African labour. The Surplus People Project (1983: 51) estimates that over a million people were forcibly relocated in Natal alone. From the early 1960s, massive forced removals began in earnest. The largest affected group consisted of labour tenants; over 300 000 people were moved as a result of farm evictions due to the abolition of labour tenancy (SPP, 1983: 53).

Commercial agriculture was divided on the abolition of labour tenancy. In Natal, farmers who farmed wattle, cattle or sheep had little use for labour tenants (Maylam, 1996: 100). However, mixed-agriculture farmers, particularly in the Natal Midlands, were concerned about the loss of labour and urged an "evolutionary" approach to the labour tenant "problem". Nevertheless, the first districts were deproclaimed[7] in June 1966, with a 1970 deadline for abolition. Many farmers claimed that they could not afford to pay the wages of full-time waged workers. The labour

---

6   Betterment planning "refers to the schemes introduced by the central government in the African reserves since the 1930s and 1940s in an attempt to control land usage and thus improve and rationalise reserve agriculture. Under betterment, tribal areas are divided into residential and agricultural land and the people living on the land [were] moved into rural villages" (Platzky & Walker, 1985: ix). However, in a fine example of Orwellian "double-speak", they actually had the opposite effect, and bettered neither the land nor people's lives.

7   This refers to the process by which the legal procedure for abolishing labour tenancy in a district is set out. "In 1964, the 1936 Development Trust and Land Act was further amended to empower the Minister of Bantu Administration to abolish entirely or to limit the system of labour tenancy in any one district of the country by proclamation" (SPP, 1983: 70–1).

tenants were alarmed at losing their livelihood and their homes, where many of them had lived for generations and where their ancestors lay buried. They did not know where they might go and what might become of their livestock.

Districts where labour tenancy was deproclaimed were thrown into turmoil. The Surplus People Project (1983: 73–90) documented the human carnage following the deproclamation in Weenen in July 1969 – a process repeated in other districts as they were deproclaimed. Large numbers of tenants resisted evictions and were forced off the farms by "hut burnings, bulldozers, arrests and prosecution"; their stock was impounded and sold through forced sales. White farmers flocked to these sales, snapping up livestock at prices much lower than their true value (SPP, 1983: 74). Many of those forcibly evicted were removed to relocation camps where conditions were squalid and facilities rudimentary. In time, many of these relocated labour tenants became the industrial workforce of the industrial decentralisation areas like Newcastle, Ladysmith and Hammarsdale (Hart, 2002: 89–95), and the factories of Pietermaritzburg and the Natal Midlands.

Other labour tenants desperately looked for alternatives to the looming evictions. They visited neighbouring farmers asking for a "place to stay", moved to already precarious and crowded black spot areas where they faced the threat of further evictions, or to reserve areas requesting the *iNkosi* to give them land (Bonnin, 1987: 87; SPP, 1983: 81). Many labour tenants on the farms of the Natal Midlands "fell under" *iNkosi* Mconjwana of Impendle, and they petitioned him for a place to stay. The influx of landless labour tenants into areas like Impendle during the 1970s contributed to land pressure, shortages and further environmental degradation in the reserves.

This was compounded by the execution of betterment schemes. Betterment planning in the Natal reserves began in the 1950s and involved the culling of cattle and the relocation of houses into rural villages (SPP, 1983: 271). Despite often violent resistance, particularly in Natal and KwaZulu, betterment schemes resulted in the relocation of 60 000 to 80 000 households (SPP, 1983: 271, 273).

The effect of this onslaught of spatial legislation was felt by the Ndlovu family and the other residents of Impendle. Because of the increasing numbers of people relocated to the area, their access to land was restricted, making it more difficult for them to support their families from the land as had their parents and grandparents. As you will read in the pages that follow, by the time Jabu married Jabulani and moved to Pietermaritzburg, her father's fields had all but disappeared, ploughed up to make way for houses; only a few fruit trees remained and the boundary fence was close to the house.

With little access to land and few jobs in the surrounding areas, young men and women like Jabu and Jabulani Ndlovu were forced to migrate to the cities to find work. Once there, they took their place among the industrial workforce. However, they were still trapped by influx control legislation, restricting access to the cities for those born in the countryside, and so the family remained in Impendle. They were like many Africans in Natal, caught between town and countryside.

Industrialisation, factory work and the city

In 1972 Jabu followed her husband to the capital of Natal, Pietermaritzburg. The distance between Impendle and Pietermaritzburg was not far, but the lifestyle and environment were very different.

In the early days of the Colony of Natal, Pietermaritzburg was the primary urban settlement servicing the surrounding agricultural areas (Stanwix, 1985: 33). It did not initially envisage itself as an industrial city, but in the late 1950s the Pietermaritzburg Chamber of Industry began pressuring the City Council to focus on industrial development (Mkhize, 1998: 13). By the early 1960s a number of industrial sites had been identified for development. To the existing industrial area of Mkhondeni was added Fitzsimons Road, Mountain Rise, Edendale Road and Woods Drive, with the Willowton industrial area developed a few years later (Mkhize, 1998: 13, 103). In 1963 the government declared Pietermaritzburg a "border industry area" (Mkhize, 1998: 103).[8] This immediately gave benefits to industry willing to locate in the city. The sectors that began to develop were food, footwear, metal and transport equipment. Between 1950 and 1970

---

8   In response to the Tomlinson Commission's (1955) recommendation, "Verwoerd argued [that] white industries requiring large numbers of African workers should be located 'in suitable European areas near Bantu territory'" (Hart, 2002: 136). The Border Industry Policy, introduced in 1960, had the distinct aim of curtailing African urbanisation. Incentives were offered to industry, including exemption from industrial council wage determinations, low-interest loans, tax concessions, transport subsidies and tariff protections. Throughout the 1960s, as forced removals and labour tenant evictions continued, the state constructed huge townships throughout the province on Bantustan land located next to the "white" areas that had been declared Border areas (Hart, 2002: 136–8).

manufacturing activity became an increasingly important part of the Natal economy, rising from 31% to 40% of regional output; after Durban, Pietermaritzburg was the most important economic region in the province (Stanwix, 1985: 35, 73).

These new industries and the employment opportunities they provided came at a time when African people living in the countryside were faced with land dispossession and relocation. As Bonnin et al (1996: 143) argue, the relocations had enormous consequences at many levels. The reserves and other parts of the countryside struggled to cope with the arrival of so many new people, which in turn had severe consequences for urbanisation. In the 1950s homesteads could produce more than half of their needs from subsistence agriculture, but by the 1970s this was reduced to less than a third (Lenta & Nattrass, cited in Bonnin et al, 1996: 143). These underlying forces pushed people from the countryside to the city.

In the cities, there were not enough houses for all the new industrial workers. So, in the late 1960s and early 1970s, the apartheid government began to develop a number of townships in Natal to accommodate urban African residents. These developments often went alongside "slum" clearance, the enforcement of the Group Areas Act, black spot removals and other spatial interventions (Hart, 2002; Bonnin, 2007; Hunter, 2010). Umlazi and KwaMashu were built in Durban for African people with urban residential rights, alongside Chatsworth and Phoenix for Indians. Mpumalanga township was built just beyond the Hammarsdale industrial area to house those industrial workers, Sundumbili township outside of Mandini was built in 1964, and Madadeni and Ezakheni were built next to Newcastle and Ladysmith. In Pietermaritzburg, the township of Imbali was developed; construction of Stage I began in 1963, followed by Stage II in the early 1970s (Mkhize, 1998: 106).

Jabu and Jabulani were part of this tide of humanity pushed towards the cities to make up the new industrial working class. With the land in Impendle increasingly unable to support the family, they moved to Pietermaritzburg in early 1972, and found accommodation in the newly built township of Imbali. In October 1974, Jabu started to work at Prestige Kitchenware (a British multinational) as an industrial worker. She was a machine operator, operating a metal press. Prestige was one of seven factories that had located itself at Mason's Mill, just next to the newly constructed Imbali township. It took advantage of the "border industry" concessions available to industry in Pietermaritzburg and was able to source its employees from the nearby township – African workers whose right to remain in the urban area was, according to influx control legislation, determined by their continued employment.

Jabu began the hard life of a production worker at the birth of what came to be known as the independent trade union movement. There was little trade union activity after the South African Congress of Trade Unions (SACTU) was driven underground in the 1960s, although workers had not forgotten what it meant to belong to a trade union (Bonnin, 1987). The re-organisation of workers in Pietermaritzburg began in the early 1970s on a number of fronts. In 1971 some students at the University of Natal in Durban started a Wages Commission to investigate the wages paid to black workers and to lobby the Wages Board for improvements (Keniston, 2013: 117). Soon a Wages

Commission started at the Pietermaritzburg campus of the University. Their first campaign focused on the wages of the unskilled black workers employed by the university, moving from there to investigate the starvation wages of workers on the wattle farms in the Natal Midlands (Merrett, forthcoming: 5). At this time African workers were not considered to be "workers" in terms of the labour legislation and were not allowed to join registered trade unions. Harriet Bolton, a Durban trade unionist, suggested the formation of the General Factory Workers' Benefit Fund (GFWBF) to provide some social services for African workers (Buhlungu, 2010: 50; Merrett, forthcoming: 7). It was founded on 9 September 1972 in Durban and soon spread to Pietermaritzburg (Merrett, forthcoming: 7).

There were also other influences in the revival of trade unionism (Buhlungu, 2010; Merrett, forthcoming: 5). Particularly important in the Pietermaritzburg area was the release of veteran SACTU unionist Harry Gwala from Robben Island in June 1972. He was given a five-year banning order, but continued to play an important role by reminding workers of the necessity of unionisation (Bonnin, 1987: 173). The first factories to join the GFWBF were metal factories, including Alcan Aluminium, Scottish Cables and Sarmcol – all factories that had long been in the area, with workers who had previously been active in trade unions (Bonnin, 1987: 175). The GFWBF had 10 000 members by the end of 1973 (Merrett, forthcoming: 8).

In January 1973 workers all over Durban went out on strike in what became known as the Durban Strikes. The strikes started at the Coronation Brick Factory on 9 January 1973 and spread rapidly to other factories, including, by the end of that month, the textile factories of Mobeni and Pinetown (IIE, 1974: 9–25). Their grievances centred around the low wages paid to factory workers. However, with the exception of a strike by 60 Alex Carriers workers, Pietermaritzburg was unaffected by the strikes (Mkhize, 1998: 107–8). This could have been, Mkhize (1998: 108–109) suggests, as a result of the large wage increases agreed to by the Pietermaritzburg City Council in February 1973.

Together, all these events led to the launch of a new union movement. On 28 April 1973, the Metal and Allied Workers Union (MAWU) was launched, the first of the new independent unions (Merrett, forthcoming: 8). At the time, it had 200 members, primarily from two factories in Pietermaritzburg – Alcan and Scottish Cables (Forrest, 2011: 11). Then the Pietermaritzburg branch of MAWU was launched on 9 June 1973, and within a year it had 1 444 members and two full-time organisers (Merrett, forthcoming: 8). In January 1974, the Trade Union Advisory and Co-ordinating Council (TUACC) was founded in MAWU's Pietermaritzburg office (Merrett, forthcoming: 8). It initially comprised MAWU and the National Union of Textile Workers (NUTW). Later, the Chemical Workers Industrial Union (CWIU) and the Transport and General Workers Union (TGWU) also joined.

The 1970s was a decade of gains and losses for the emerging independent union movement. By mid-1974 MAWU had signed up 3 883 members in at least 68 factories (Forrest, 2011: 15). But as much as the unions endeavoured to organise workers, so management resisted and the state attempted to smash their efforts. Management refused to meet union representatives, and actively promoted liaison committees in their factories. The independent unions struggled to organise workers. In 1974 Moses Mbanjwa and Jeannette Cunningham-Brown, MAWU organisers in Pietermaritzburg, were banned. In 1976 the state once more banned a number of trade union organisers, including most of the leadership of MAWU and the NUTW (Bonnin et al, 1996: 155). Facing collapse, MAWU developed a new organising strategy. At its core were careful decisions around which plants to organise, and the infiltration of shop stewards onto the liaison committees. Slowly membership was built again (Friedman, 1987; Bonnin et al, 1996; Forrest, 2011; Merrett, forthcoming).

In April 1979 a new union federation – the Federation of South African Trade Unions (FOSATU) – was formed. MAWU was one of the founding members. FOSATU's principles were non-racialism, worker control and leadership, factory-floor strength and the shop steward system, broad-based autonomous industrial unions and tight financial controls (Merrett, forthcoming: 11).

It was not easy for a worker to be a union member at this time. A survey of workers conducted by Edward Webster and Judson Khuzwayo showed that workers "were afraid of dismissal and police action, believing that the state would associate labour activism with the ANC" (Forrest, 2011: 16). Jabu was working at Prestige during this time. She would have been aware of the police harassment of workers who were associated with unions. She would have seen the breaking of the Conac Engineering strike in 1975 and noticed that, despite the law limiting overtime, workers who went on strike over this issue were dismissed (Merrett, forthcoming: 9). She would have read about the banning of union officials in 1976, and the deaths in detention. She would have known that MAWU organiser Moses Ndlovu, who was associated with ANC members and offered support to their families, was banned.

Production work was demanding, the hours were long, the wages low and the working conditions harsh. As this book explains, workers at Prestige were often badly treated – overtime was not fairly paid, there was little regard for health and safety, jobs were insecure and workers had no legal protection. In 1981 MAWU organisers John Makhathini and Geoff Schreiner started to recruit workers at Prestige. Jabu was among the first to join. In 1983, soon after MAWU signed a recognition agreement with Prestige, she was elected a shop steward; in 1985 she became a senior shop steward. Prestige was one of the strongest of MAWU's Pietermaritzburg factories and contributed to the growth of the union movement in the area at that time (Sitas, 1983). A key strategy in this growth was plant-level bargaining, which allowed the union to negotiate wage increases significantly higher than those granted by the Industrial Council (Sitas, 1983: 1).

Jabu's story allows us to understand the sacrifices that were made by shop stewards in building the independent trade union movement. Shop stewards were the heart of the trade unions. When the state moved to suppress the trade union movement in the 1970s and it seemed as if the independent unions were going to be crushed, union officials decided that the members and worker leaders should be the foundation upon which the unions would be built. Kally Forrest described their role in her book about the National Union of Metalworkers of South Africa (NUMSA)[9] – "Shop stewards played a central role

---

9   In 1985 (in accordance with COSATU's "One Industry One Union" principle), MAWU merged with other metal unions to form the National Union of Metalworkers of South Africa.

and were directly accountable to members, organising in their departments and dealing with management. They also represented members on MAWU's Branch Executive Committee" (Forrest, 2011: 15). Besides acting as the face of the union in the factory, shop stewards also represented members on many different structures and consequently attended many meetings, usually after working hours. Jabu forfeited time with her family in the evenings and over the weekends to help build the union movement. In time shop steward structures united factories and workers across regions. Forrest (2011: 49–53) describes the emergence of the Shop Stewards Councils and their significant contribution to the growth of MAWU. The first Shop Stewards Council was formed in Pietermaritzburg in 1982, and in time this structure was replicated across the country. Not only did they unite factories across a region and between sectors, but they also allowed for the "creation of a powerful grassroots movement" (Forrest, 2011: 51).

The early 1980s was a time of fierce struggle and organisation. The union movement, including MAWU, was growing rapidly in many parts of the country. By the end of 1981, FOSATU was the largest union group in the country with 95 000 members in 387 organised factories (Baskin, 1991: 29). However, while workers wanted to join the unions, managements were not particularly eager to negotiate or to sign recognition agreements. Many of the strikes of this time were about union recognition, although they also fought for better wages and against dismissals (Howe, 1984: 5). In 1983 more than 54 recognition agreements were signed countrywide, including with Prestige and Scottish Cable in Pietermaritzburg (Howe, 1984: 9).

Many of the wage demands (and strikes) were fuelled

by the economic recession of the early to mid-1980s. In 1982 Pietermaritzburg was once more declared an industrial deconcentration point,[10] and by 1984 the manufacturing sector employed 20 000 workers, significant for Pietermaritzburg but small in comparison to Durban's 200 000 (LMG, 1985: 90). The growth of employment, driven by the state's industrialisation policy, was offset by the recession, and unemployment remained very high. A number of factories (Feralloys, Dick Whittington Shoes, Sarmcol) retrenched staff, with close to 2 000 jobs being lost. Unemployment among blacks was estimated at 36%, with about 80% of these under 35 years of age (Mkhize, 1998: 114). Mkhize (1998) argues that the political mobilisation of the youth during the 1980s needs to be understood against the high youth unemployment.

Jabu's story also demonstrates the politics that was developing among MAWU members and shop stewards at the time. Jabu did not have a narrow view of the role of the trade union; she did not see it as an organisation only concerned with the workplace. In Pietermaritzburg, she was at the forefront of the struggles of workers, youth, communities and women. She sat on shop steward structures; she participated in the Prestige Choir and performed at many cultural events; she was a church

---

10 From the late 1970s, the apartheid government began to rethink its Border Industry Policy, and in 1982, announced its "new" Regional Decentralisation Strategy. This economic plan divided South Africa into eight development regions; within these regions were eleven deconcentration points (areas close to existing large metropolitan areas) and 49 industrial development points. Incentive packages were offered to attract labour-intensive industry to these areas. A major difference between this Strategy and the Border Industry incentives was a move away from tax concessions to cash payments based on the number of workers employed (Zille, 1983: 58–60).

member; she participated in the NUMSA Women's Forum and in women's organisations outside of union structures; and she involved herself in the community, particularly with the youth. Jabu understood that these different areas were all linked in the oppression of black women workers.

The role of trade unions was hotly debated within the union movement and political groups at the time. Jabu's commitment arose as a result of the daily struggle in which she was engaged. Key to this was the Sarmcol strike of May 1985. Sarmcol workers went on strike over union recognition, and within three days the entire workforce was dismissed (Bonnin, 1987). As part of the campaign for reinstatement, they organised a boycott of white shops in the Howick area. This boycott soon spread to Pietermaritzburg and was followed by a worker stayaway on 18 July 1985, organised with the support of youth organisations (LMG, 1985; Bonnin, 1987). The Shop Stewards Council played an important role in the organisation and consultation with community organisations.

Jabu became more prominent in MAWU and NUMSA campaigns that involved engagement with the broader community. Prestige workers organised a lunch-time demonstration to draw attention to the detention without trial of Johannesburg NUMSA organiser Moses Mayekiso. Jabu also supported the Sarmcol struggle cultural group, Sisters of the Long March, and travelled overseas with them as part of the campaign to raise awareness around Mayekiso's detention and the Sarmcol struggle. This, together with her public support for youth organisations in the Pietermaritzburg area, brought her to the attention of the Inkatha Freedom Party at a time when the civil war between United Democratic Front (UDF) affiliates and Inkatha was intensifying, and she began to receive death threats.

Civil war in Natal

In November 1985, after years of negotiations, FOSATU and independent unions from different traditions merged to form the Congress of South African Trade Unions (COSATU). Relations between the independent unions and Inkatha had become strained, but this turned into outright hostility after the formation of COSATU (Bonnin et al, 1996: 158–60). Inkatha opposed the strikes and stayaways called by COSATU-affiliated unions, and there were often violent clashes. In Pietermaritzburg, COSATU members, particularly bus drivers, were targeted by Inkatha as the result of the May 1986 stayaway (Kentridge, 1990). But it was the attack on the Sarmcol strike leadership and the community of Mpophomeni (home of the majority of the strikers) by Inkatha-linked vigilantes on 5 December 1986 that brought the conflict to the heart of the NUMSA and COSATU Shop Stewards Councils. Phineas Sibiya, one of those murdered, was a senior shop steward at Sarmcol and a long-time member of both Shop Stewards Councils.

The tensions, sometimes violent, between UDF-aligned structures, unions and Inkatha had turned to sustained violence in the wake of the murder on 1 August 1985 of Victoria Mxenge, a member of the Natal UDF executive and the Natal Organisation of Women. There was a continual escalation in the number of deaths and arson cases in most of the African townships around Pietermaritzburg. But from

September 1987, there was a sharp peak in murders, and 60 deaths were reported. For the next three years this level of killing was maintained (Aitchison, 1988; Bonnin, 2007).

In different places there were different dynamics to the violence, but over the next six years (and beyond) the violent conflict and death spread through the province like wildfire. In some places the conflict appeared generational, in others it seemed to be about land and resources, while in other areas it hooked onto historical disputes. Despite these different dynamics, in most places the conflict was between men loyal to Inkatha and youth associated with UDF-affiliated youth congresses. As the violence monitoring records show, the majority of those killed were young men (Aitchison, 1988).

Bonnin (2007: 15) describes the process that occurred in most areas. The skirmishes that began among the youth soon involved other members of their households as the political affiliation of the male youth transferred to the entire household. Households that were not deemed to have the "correct" political affiliation or who were seen to be harbouring the enemy were attacked. The occupants were killed or forced to flee. Areas became associated with either Inkatha or the UDF, and they became "no-go" zones for those associated with the other side. The violence reorganised the geography of the Natal countryside, and in the process branded political identities onto particular areas.

Pietermaritzburg and its surrounding areas became the epicentre of the escalating violence during 1987. Inkatha had not been able to find overwhelming support in the Pietermaritzburg townships, as shown by the support provided, against Inkatha's wishes, to the BTR Sarmcol strikers (Gwala, 1989). In 1987 they began a recruitment campaign in order to win back support, and were fiercely resisted. The surge in violence was attributed to this (Gwala, 1989). By the end of 1987, Inkatha was losing the battle in the Pietermaritzburg area, and the security forces stepped in on the side of Inkatha. The notorious Caprivi trainees[11] and special constables,[12] also known as *kitskonstabels*, were deployed to assist Inkatha (Kentridge, 1990: Bonnin, 2007). According to Jac Buchner, head of

---

11 In November 1985, Mangosuthu Buthelezi, Chief Minister of the KwaZulu Homeland and President of Inkatha, approached the apartheid state for military support that would include an offensive or attacking capacity. South Africa's State Security Council approved the creation of a covert paramilitary unit to support Inkatha. Recruitment was from existing Inkatha members, often using well-known warlords to select men on the ground. Approximately 200 men in their late teens and early twenties were chosen. In June 1986, they were secretly flown to the Caprivi Strip in Namibia. They received training at the Hippo Camp by the Special Operations component of Military Intelligence and the Special Forces. Here, they were placed under the command of Duluxolo Luthuli. Once the training was completed, they were infiltrated back into different communities throughout the province where they played a covert role in stoking the violence. MZ Khumalo, Inkatha secretary-general, played a central role in launching offensive actions, including identifying the targets for elimination and supplying the trainees with arms and ammunition. One of the first offensive operations undertaken by the Caprivi trainees was the KwaMakhutha massacre in January 1987 (Bonnin 1987: 207–17).

12 At the beginning of 1988, Buthelezi asked for more Inkatha members to be trained in order to swing the conflict in the townships in his favour. Responding to this pressure and Inkatha's complaints that the South African Police were biased in favour of the UDF, special constables were recruited into the SAP. As with the Caprivi trainees, only loyal Inkatha men were considered. The special constables came from two sources – new recruits and the Caprivi trainees. No checks were done to ensure that the recruits had a clear criminal record. The special constables received six weeks' training at Koeberg in the Cape, including the use of shotguns and 9 mm pistols. As in the Caprivi training, there was a large measure of indoctrination. Upon completion of their training they were integrated into the SAP, the majority of them initially deployed in the Pietermaritzburg area. They were informed that their job was to assist Inkatha (Bonnin, 1987: 213–17).

the Security Branch in Pietermaritzburg, the police had been able to "restore a certain sense of law and order by February [1988]" (Smith, 1992: 244). However, the UDF-aligned youth soon reorganised and by the end of the year the violence was as bad as before. And it continued that way well into the early 1990s.

Jabu's story gives us a window into the experiences of ordinary women during the time of violence. Her eldest son, Linda, became involved in the Congress of South African Students (COSAS). In 1985 Inkatha members began to attack COSAS members at Linda's school in Ashdown and he was forced to flee from the school. He then joined the Imbali Youth Organisation. Soon, like many of the other youth, he was in hiding, rarely sleeping at home; the police and *kitskonstabels* frequently raided the family's house looking for Linda. Jabu, like other mothers, sent her younger children away so that they could continue schooling, as most of the schools had closed as a consequence of the violence. As we learn in the book, her involvement in the struggle meant that she was respected by the youth.

COSATU was at the forefront of attempts to bring about peace in Pietermaritzburg. Numerous rounds of talks were held between COSATU, the UDF and Inkatha, but each attempt to bring about agreement seemed to end in further conflict or repression (Baskin, 1991). Eventually, an accord was reached in September 1988 and a Complaints Adjudication Board was established, but it had little success and COSATU soon suspended its involvement. The violence had a devastating impact on COSATU and its structures. Many union members living in Inkatha areas were forced to flee their homes;

bus drivers in Pietermaritzburg were a particular target. Workers complained that they were continually tired from having to stay awake all night defending their homes from attack and then having to work a full day. Attendance at COSATU locals and other union meetings dropped as workers wanted to go straight home from work because it was more dangerous to travel at night. Many unionists throughout Natal were targeted; they were shot at, their families harassed and their houses burned (Forrest, 2011: 376–81).

COSATU continued to work for peace. It set up a working group that gathered information and affidavits about the violence. Its 1989 "Report on the Natal Violence" demonstrated the partisan nature of the police, showing how they were reluctant to intervene in incidents of violence or to prosecute perpetrators. The report also detailed the forced recruitment campaigns of Inkatha and their use of armed vigilante groups. And it noted that UDF supporters were becoming increasingly undisciplined and engaging in cycles of revenge killing. All of this, the report said, alienated the community (Kentridge, 1990: 339; Forrest, 2011: 386–7). COSATU and the UDF then called for a peace conference to bring together a diverse group of people and organisations to discuss peace. But Buthelezi rejected this initiative, and the violence and killing continued.

Jabu was a member of the working group that produced the COSATU report. As we read in the pages that follow, the first case documented in the dossier was that of her son Linda. Soon after the release of the report, Jabu's home in Imbali was attacked and firebombed. Jabu's husband Jabulani and her daughter Khumbu were killed in the attack; Jabu was severely injured, and died ten days later in hospital. Another of Jabu's daughters, Luhle, and her nephew, Thabane, who were also in the house, were wounded but escaped with their lives.

Conclusion

Ultimately Jabu's story is one of courage – courage in a time of oppression and violence that birthed our democracy, and one that should not be forgotten. The struggles she fought still resonate with us today.

First, the specific events that affected Jabu's family are embedded in the wider history of colonial conquest and apartheid. As a result of apartheid, Jabu's family lost the land that had been given to her grandfather to build his *umuzi* and to sustain his family. The process of land restitution has still not been resolved, and for many families it remains a bitter reminder of how apartheid still affects their lives today.

Second, at a time when the union movement is divided and many workers feel that union leaders are far removed from their daily struggles, Jabu's story reminds us that the shop stewards as worker leaders played a key role in building and sustaining that movement. They were the lodestone in creating a strong union movement able to fight to improve the conditions of workers both inside and outside the factory.

Third, in a time when leadership comes with the expectation of material rewards, Jabu's story allows us to reflect on the sacrifices that she and others made in the struggle to create a different society built on different values.

She and other worker and community leaders sacrificed their family time, personal freedom and, ultimately, their lives without reward or the expectation of higher office.

Fourth, at a time when political killings in KwaZulu-Natal are on the rise again, her story reminds us of the devastation that violence brings to families, communities and organisations. The politics and dynamics behind the violence today are not the same as in the 1980s and early 1990s, but the need remains for strong and moral leaders like Jabu to speak out and organise against the violence and the moral corruption that lies behind it.

Read this book and be inspired!

REFERENCES

Aitchison, J. (1988) Numbering the Dead. Unpublished mimeo.

Baskin, J. (1991) *Striking Back: A History of COSATU.* Johannesburg: Ravan Press.

Bonnin, D. (1987) Class, Consciousness and Conflict in the Natal Midlands, 1940–1987: The Case of the BTR Sarmcol Workers. Master of Social Science dissertation, University of Natal, Durban.

Bonnin, D. (2007) Space, Place and Identity: Political Violence in Mpumalanga Township, KwaZulu-Natal, 1987–1993. PhD dissertation, University of the Witwatersrand, Johannesburg.

Bonnin, D., G. Hamilton, R. Morrell and A. Sitas (1996) The Struggle for Natal and KwaZulu: Workers, Township Dwellers and Inkatha, 1972–1985. In *Political Economy and Identities in KwaZulu-Natal: Historical and Social Perspectives,* edited by R. Morrell. Durban: Indicator Press.

Buhlungu, S. (2010) *A Paradox of Victory. COSATU and the Democratic Transformation in South Africa.* Pietermaritzburg: University of KwaZulu-Natal Press.

Carton, B. (2000) *Blood from Your Children. The Colonial Origins of Generational Conflict in South Africa.* Pietermaritzburg: University of KwaZulu-Natal Press.

Christopher, A. (1968) Natal: A Study in Colonial Land Settlement. PhD dissertation, University of Natal, Durban.

Forrest, K. (2011) *Metal That Will Not Bend. National Union of Metalworkers of South Africa, 1980–1995.* Johannesburg: Wits University Press.

Friedman, S. (1987) *Building Tomorrow Today: African Workers in Trade Unions 1970–1984.* Johannesburg: Ravan Press.

Guy, J. (1997) An Accommodation of Patriarchs: Theophilus Shepstone and the Foundation of the System of Native Administration in Natal. Paper presented to the International Colloquium on Masculinities, University of Natal, July.

Guy, J. (2006) *Remembering the Rebellion. The Zulu Uprising of 1906.* Pietermaritzburg: University of KwaZulu-Natal Press.

Guy, J. (2013) *Theophilus Shepstone and the Forging of Natal.* Pietermaritzburg: University of KwaZulu-Natal Press.

Gwala, N. [B.E. Nzimande] (1989) Political Violence and the Struggle for Control in Pietermaritzburg. *Journal of Southern African Studies*, 15(3): 506–524.

Hart, G. (2002) *Disabling Globalization: Places of Power in Post-Apartheid South Africa.* Pietermaritzburg: University of KwaZulu-Natal Press.

Howe, G. (1984) Strike Trend Indicators 1982–1984. *Indicator SA*, 2: 3–9.

Hunter, M. (2010) *Love in the Time of AIDS: Inequality, Gender and Rights in South Africa.* Pietermaritzburg: University of KwaZulu-Natal Press.

Institute for Industrial Education (IIE) (1974) *The Durban Strikes 1973.* Durban: Institute for Industrial Education and Ravan Press.

Keniston, K. (2013) *Choosing to be Free: The Life Story of Rick Turner.* Johannesburg: Jacana.

Kentridge, M. (1990) *An Unofficial War: Inside the Conflict in Pietermaritzburg.* Cape Town: David Philip.

Labour Monitoring Group (LMG) (1985) Monitoring the Sarmcol Struggle. *South African Labour Bulletin*. 11(2): 89–112.

Lambert, J. and R. Morrell (1996) Domination and Subordination in Natal, 1890–1920. In *Political Economy and Identities in KwaZulu-Natal: Historical and Social Perspectives,* edited by R. Morrell. Durban: Indicator Press.

Marks, S. (1970) *Reluctant Rebellion. The 1906–1908 Disturbances in Natal.* London: Oxford University Press.

Maylam, P. (1996) The Changing Political Economy of the Region, 1920–1950. In *Political Economy and Identities in KwaZulu-Natal: Historical and Social Perspectives,* edited by R. Morrell. Durban: Indicator Press.

Merrett, C. (forthcoming) Masters and Servants: Black Trade Unions in Pietermaritzburg and the Natal Midlands before the mid-1980s. *Natalia.*

Mkhize, S. (1998) Contexts, Resistance Crowds and Mass Mobilisation: A Comparative Analysis of Anti-Apartheid Politics in Pietermaritzburg during the 1950s and the 1980s. Master of Arts dissertation, University of Natal, Pietermaritzburg.

Morrell, R., J. Wright and S. Meintjes (1996) Colonialism and the Establishment of White Domination, 1840–1890. In *Political Economy and Identities in KwaZulu-Natal: Historical and Social Perspectives,* edited by R. Morrell. Durban: Indicator Press.

Platzky, L. and C. Walker (1985) *The Surplus People: Forced Removals in South Africa.* Johannesburg: Ravan Press.

Sitas, A. (1983) MAWU: Rapid Growth in Natal. *South African Labour Bulletin,* 8(8) & 9(1): 1–2.

Slater, H. (1980) Changing Economic Relationships in Rural Natal. In *Economy and Society in Pre-Industrial South Africa,* edited by S. Marks and A. Atmore. London and New York: Longman.

Smith, T. (1992) Trust Feed wasn't a One-off Massacre. In *Patterns of Violence. Case Studies of Conflict in Natal,* edited by A. Minnaar. Pretoria: HSRC.

Stanwix, J. (1985) A Study of the Natal Regional Economy. Natal Town and Regional Planning Report, Vol. 66. Pietermaritzburg: Natal Town and Regional Planning

Commission.

Surplus People Project (SPP) (1983) *Forced Removals in South Africa: Natal, Vol 4 of the Surplus People Project Reports.* Cape Town: Surplus People Project.

Zille, H. (1983) Restructuring the Industrial Decentralisation Strategy. In *South African Review One: Same Foundations, New Facades?* edited by South African Research Service. Johannesburg: Ravan Press.

Introduction to the first edition

PEOPLE IN IMBALI SAY THE WAR started in 1985. Before then, the community of Imbali had only seen the violent upheavals that have been part of South Africa since 1976 on TV. For them, violence was something that happened to other people in other towns.

Imbali was the township where Jabu Ndlovu lived with her family and children. Today, Jabu is dead. Her husband, eldest daughter and eldest son are also dead. Four children have survived the war. They live scattered in different parts of the country.

Like thousands of other families, the Ndlovu family has been destroyed by the war. Like thousands of other homes, theirs stands empty, the roof caved in, the walls blackened by fire, windows and doors smashed, the garden overrun with weeds.

In 1985 war broke out between the United Democratic Front (UDF) and Inkatha in Natal. The townships around Pietermaritzburg, including Imbali, were among the worst hit.

Many of those affected have been ordinary people – people who would say they were "neutral" in the struggle. But the Ndlovu family was not neutral. Jabu Ndlovu was a loved and respected trade unionist and community leader and UDF supporter. Her eldest son, Linda, had joined other UDF supporters – "Comrades" – in forming teams to defend the community against attacks by Inkatha supporters.

It was inevitable that the Ndlovu family would become a target of violence. Their attackers were the "vigilantes" – armed men fighting for Inkatha. The vigilante leaders have become known as warlords. These are men who hold great power in the townships because they command these vigilante "armies", and because they are often landowners or officials in KwaZulu state structures.

As Jabu's story unfolds, you will see how the people of Imbali tried to fight back against the warlords. Jabu was one of the many leaders who accused the police of supporting the warlords and the vigilantes and turning a blind eye to their brutality.

A typical attack

The attack on Jabu's home was typical of attacks in the Natal civil war. The house was attacked after midnight by men armed with guns. They forced entry and shot whoever they could find. They then set the house alight and tried to kill others as they fled from the flames. Jabu survived the attack, with a bullet wound and severe burns. She lived for only ten days – just long enough to name her killers before she died.

When Jabu died, the whole community mourned. Her union, the National Union of Metalworkers of South Africa (NUMSA) and community leaders called a stayaway. Workers from Imbali and other places went on strike.

Jabu's death inspired NUMSA to set up a Trust Fund in her name, to provide for the education of her children as well as for the education of other children who have been orphaned by the war – the children in the refugee camps or living on the streets, who will be victims of the war long after the peace is won.

In setting up the Trust, the union said, "There are many other children who have been deprived and who now live on the streets. This will not happen to Jabu's children because she was an important and well-known leader, and the union will see to it that they are taken care of. Jabu would have expected this support from us. But she would also have asked, 'What about the other children who have faced this problem?'"

In the same spirit, we have written this book. Money from its sale will go towards the future of Jabu's children and the children of the many others who have died.

But we have also told Jabu's story to explore the suffering and courage of communities ravaged by the war, and especially to tell the stories of the women who have struggled, fought and died.

Today, over a year after her death, people still mourn and miss Jabu – her family, her friends and the workers of the factory whom she represented as a shop steward. These are the people who told us her story.

In telling Jabu's story, in the words of the people who knew and loved her, we hope to show how she struggled as a woman, a member of the community and as a worker for freedom and peace in South Africa. Her experience was that of thousands of others who have struggled and suffered as a result of the war. Through her story, we hope also to share their experiences.

My message is to encourage the women to struggle, even if they are not working, to be active within the community. They must help the community, especially the youth – help them when they have got problems.

The youth complain that their fathers are not helping, especially on the weekends they go off drinking. So the women must help the youth – they must call meetings and help them plan what to do.

– JABU NDLOVU

ONE
A gifted child

"I'M GETTING GIRLS ONLY ... GIRLS ONLY," Jabu's father complained when she was born. Jabu was the third daughter. She was born at Nhlabamkhosi in Impendle "native reserve" on 25 March 1947. She was christened Jabulile Florence.

Mothers in Impendle say children could not be born unless Jabu's mother, Ina Zuma, was present. Ina was a birth attendant in the district. She had not been trained as a midwife and says her talent for helping mothers bring their babies into the world was "a gift from God".

Ina bore seven children, four girls and three boys. Because of her gift, she needed very little assistance when the time came for her own children to be born. She remembers cutting the umbilical cord of her second daughter, Noma, without aid. But for the other children there were women in attendance while, according to the custom, the men waited outside.

Ina was the daughter of farmworkers living on a white-owned farm in the Natal Midlands. Like thousands of African families living in the "white areas" of South Africa, where they could not own land, her family were tenant farmers. They would work for the farmer for six months of the year in return for the right to use a small piece of land where they could plant crops and graze cattle for the remaining six months.

Ina remembers her meeting with Jabu's father, Phambano Petrus Mkhize. "I am from Mthulini, near Nottingham Road. I was working on a farm called Nzinga and later I went to Loteni. We met through his travelling. He came there, and in 1939 we got married. Then we went to live with his mother at Nhlabamkhosi at Impendle, because she was a widow and because in those days a wife was not allowed to work. We stayed there with his family, in houses they had built under the mountain. We started our family there."

The house where Jabu was born had been built by her grandfather, who was a policeman in Impendle. Impendle is the name of a small area which was demarcated a "reserve" area for African occupation by the Natal Colonial Government in the early 1900s. It is in the heart of the fertile Natal Midlands and was given to Africans because it was unsuitable for farming. The people know it as a place of hills, rocks and "the great wind" – *Inkanyamba.*

Phambano was the eldest of the Mkhize children. His family moved to Impendle after his birth in 1911. The chief granted them fields at Nhlabamkhosi and they settled there to farm with cattle and vegetables. This was the place where Jabu was born.

Phambano has to work

When Phambano was only 12, his father died, leaving very little money. As the eldest son, he had to leave school to find work to help his mother feed and educate his brothers and sisters. He first looked for work close to home, and managed to earn some money doing odd-jobs for the farmer and for Catholic mission stations in the district. But the money was not enough and by the time he was 15, Phambano had left Impendle to seek work in Durban.

It was 1926, and even in those days Durban was the fastest-growing town in Natal. Phambano quickly found work on a building site as a handyman.

While he was employed there, a fellow worker encouraged Phambano to become a Roman Catholic. Phambano was strongly attracted to the religion and after going to many sermons at a church near the site where he worked, and consulting with the priest, he agreed to be baptised. He spent long hours studying the texts of the faith and later became the priest's server. That is how Jabu and her brothers and sisters came to be brought up as Catholics.

Jabu's religion was very important to her and many years later she followed her father's example. She became active in the church by joining the Mothers' Union, and all her own children were baptised and went to Roman Catholic schools.

After working in Durban for a few years, Phambano heard that a clinic was to be built near Bulwer – a town close to his family home. He applied for a job and was employed as a labourer at the site. There he learned bricklaying and woodwork.

Jabu's mother, Ina Mkhize, at Gomane.

When the clinic was finished, Phambano was on the move again. Jobs were scarce in the rural areas and he had to travel long distances in search of work. Along the way he stopped at Loteni, and that, as Ina says, is how they met.

The couple's first-born – Jabu's big sister – was Thoko. The next-born was Noma, and then came Jabu. Thoko was six years older than Jabu and she remembers looking after her when she was a baby while her parents were working in the fields. Like many elder sisters, Thoko looked after all of her younger brothers and sisters.

As his family grew, Phambano decided that he wanted to be self-employed. He wanted to try and earn a living from farming. The house at Nhlabamkhosi was on a steep slope and the ground was stony. So Phambano applied to Chief Mconjwana Zuma for a plot across the valley at Gomane. He was allocated a piece of land, and while Jabu was still a toddler, the family left their grandmother's house and moved to Gomane.

The new house was not too far from their old one. From the stoep of their new home, the children could still see the place where they had been born.

Life at Gomane

At Gomane, the children led carefree lives playing with their neighbours. "Jabu was the most active of all of us," says Thoko. "I remember she used to like to play football outside with the other children. And she used to like to play *ingqathu* – skipping – with the other girls. She used to forget even to cook when she was skipping."

Noma, the second sister, was two years older than Jabu.

She remembers playing *umacashelana* – hide-and-seek – with her in the long grass on the hillside, until their mother stopped them because of the snakes. Noma also remembers Jabu's closeness with Dumisani, the next-born. Jabu and her brother used to play outside for as long as possible. But their father was strict and would always call them inside before the sun set.

Because he had to leave school to go to work, Phambano wanted more than anything to educate his children. "He used to say when we are all educated we are going to look after ourselves," says Thoko. "In our family, if we didn't finish school, it was because we failed. You never heard my father say you must stop going to school. He wanted everybody to get educated."

The money for the children's education came from Phambano's fields and from his cattle. In the old days, Thoko remembers, the Mkhize family had about 70 cattle, and in the fields around the house they had planted fruit trees as well as potatoes, peas, mealies and other vegetables.

"We had a lot of ground around our home where my father used to plough," says Thoko. "There were no houses there, like now. One year he used to plant potatoes, and the next year he used to change and plant mealies, and then rotate again."

In summer, after Phambano had ploughed, the whole family worked in the fields. "Whatever we did, we did in the morning before we went to school. Then after school, when we came out, one of us would cook and one would go and help my mother in the fields, planting or picking. Another would collect the cattle from outside and bring them into the kraal," Thoko remembers. When the boys were old enough, they took over the job of herding the cattle, while the girls had to concentrate on learning housework and cooking.

In winter, Phambano worked as a carpenter, making and selling furniture. His work was in demand and he enlisted the help of the whole family in varnishing and sanding. "We all used to be busy at home during the weekends. We used to enjoy doing it because we knew that if people had ordered, say, a dining room suite, we know that money would come in when the customer came to collect. He made so much furniture that he kept some of it. We still have some of the things he made here at home," says Noma.

The children also helped their grandmother at Nhlabamkhosi making grass mats. Thoko and Noma remember spending many hours with Jabu over weekends sorting the grasses into long and short pieces, and counting out piles of mats, which would be bought by couples when they got married.

"Our grandmother used to sell them and buy presents for us – clothing, school uniforms. She used to go to Impendle village to buy, and when we came home there would be a parcel for us," says Thoko.

The three sisters go to school

Ina Zuma prepared her children well for school. Before her marriage, she used to work on different farms, planting and harvesting, and in her spare time she used to teach the children of other farmworkers English.

Today if you ask Mama Mkhize about her teaching she just laughs, but Thoko remembers how this made the Mkhize children luckier than some of their neighbours.

Mama Mkhize used to teach them basic English to prepare them for school. "She used to teach us that the first words at school are a, e, i, o, u," says Thoko.

When they turned seven, the Mkhize daughters were sent to a Roman Catholic mission school, Clairvoux Mission, which was 25 kilometres away from their home. Phambano chose Clairvoux Mission for his children because it was the closest Catholic school. In those days the church did not approve of Catholics going to non-Catholic schools.

Thoko, Noma and Jabu all started there, as boarders. Noma remembers that the school had many students because it did not only take Catholics. It was also famous in other parts of South Africa. "There were even children from Johannesburg," says Noma. "And they were happy if children from the other churches came as well, because they knew they would change to become Catholics."

Clairvoux Mission, with its impressive steeple and four giant bells, was also the church the Mkhize family attended on Sundays. People walked great distances to come to Clairvoux Mission and outside the church there is a shallow pool where they used to wash the sweat and dust off their feet before going inside to pray. Today the pool is no longer in use: when the bells ring out across the valley on Sundays, many in the congregation come in cars or public transport.

During term time, the children did not often go home, says Noma. "Our parents were not allowed to take us out of school for weekends, unless it was for a serious matter. We used to see them every Sunday, although at times they couldn't both come. But if one was there we were happy."

Jabu was lucky to have her big sisters to look after her when she arrived at Clairvoux. "We were many in our dormitory," says Noma. "All the girls were in one dormitory and all the boys in another. And since we were very young, we had the older girls to watch over us, and even wash us at times. The teachers used to look after us, too. They were strict, but I can see that they were taking the part of our parents. So if we were dirty, they used to tell us, 'No, you should go and wash and change'."

After a time, the Roman Catholic Church relaxed its attitude and the three sisters started going to Gomane Primary School, which was only a 30-minute walk from their home.

"She used to come out number one."

Mama Mkhize says Jabu was very bright at school. "She never failed at school. She was cleverer than all my other children. I think she was gifted."

Thoko and Noma agree. "She liked to do arithmetic, and when she came back from school she always used to take her books and read and write. She used to come out number one in exams. She was clever, very clever," says Thoko. She continued, "She used to like playing basketball – in fact, anything that was being played. I remember once, when she was about 14, she broke her arm playing. She had a fracture of the right arm, and it was put in plaster of Paris for about six months. I remember in those days to put plaster of Paris was a terrible sight to see."

From Gomane, Jabu went to Nxamalala Secondary School at Sithunjwana, which is an area of Impendle. The school had just opened and the Mkhize children were among its first pupils. Nxamalala had only four rooms – one

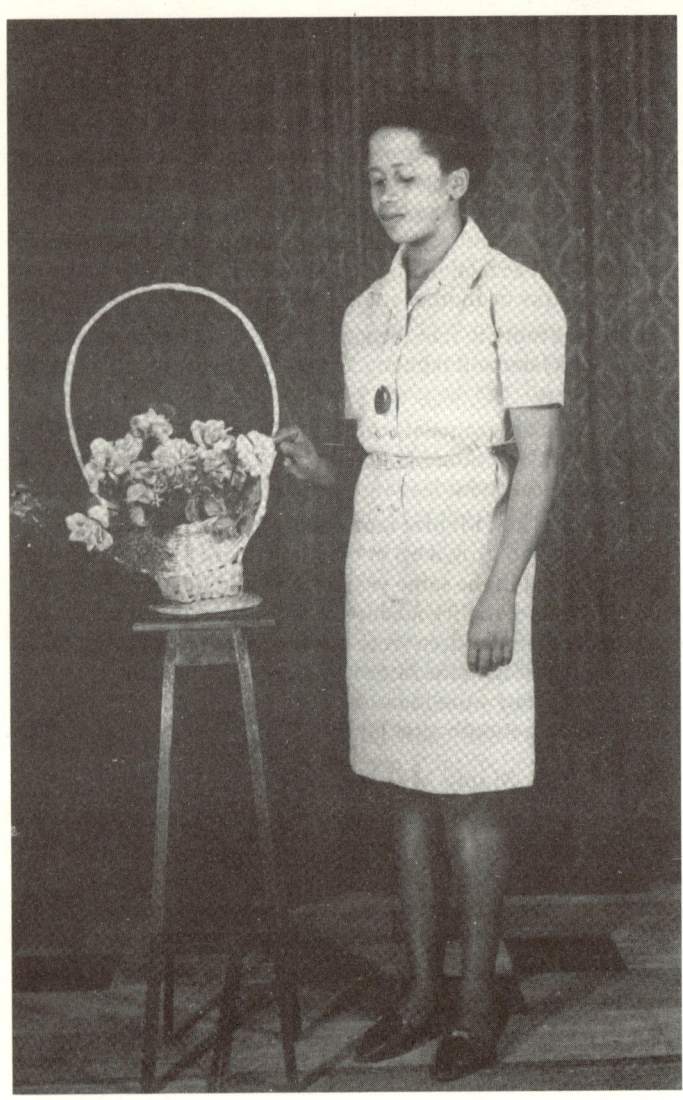

Jabu in her teens. At 17, she fell in love with Jabulani.

for each form – when Jabu started there, and a staffroom. The school was in the bushes, Thoko recalls. "Today there is a new school with many more classrooms. No electricity – that is a dream – but there are two big fields, one for football and the other for basketball."

At Nxamalala, Jabu still came first in class. But there was some tough competition from a classmate, Jabulani Ndlovu. Noma remembers this classroom struggle: "I heard from classmates that they were competing in class. In fact, they were both clever and I understand that if Jabu got the highest marks in a certain subject, Jabulani used to work hard so that he could get more marks in another subject."

There was more to this struggle than just competition over marks. Soon Jabu and Jabulani admitted they were in love and became lovers.

Jabu stayed at Nxamalala until she completed Standard 8 [Grade 10]. The school did not offer Standard 9 or 10 in those days, but Jabu had another reason for leaving: she was pregnant with Khumbu.

The Ndlovu and Mkhize families had always been very close because they had grown up in the same district. Phambano and Ina got married in the same year as the Ndlovus, and they expressed their good friendship by calling each other *mlingani* even before their children were born. Normally only couples who have children of the same age call each other *mlingani*. As it turned out, they were to become *mlingani* – Jabulani was born just over a month after Jabu.

A surprise for Mama Mkhize

The children's relationship still came as a surprise to Mama Mkhize. "We do not know how they came together. Long after we had forgotten about them being born together and knowing each other, we heard the Ndlovus were coming to pay *lobola*. We thought that God had planned it to be like that," she says.

Mama Mkhize became Gogo Mkhize, a grandmother, in 1965, when her first granddaughter, Khumbu, was born.

When Khumbu was a few months old, Jabulani left Impendle to look for work in Pietermaritzburg. Work was hard to find at Impendle and most of the young men used to go to Pietermaritzburg or Durban, says Gogo Mkhize.

During this period, Jabu stayed with her parents to look after Khumbu. She was also teaching. Gomane Primary School was short of staff and the principal asked her father if she could work there as a private teacher. At the same time, Jabu registered with Damelin College in Johannesburg, hoping to complete her matric through correspondence. But, Noma recalls, she had taken on too much. "It was too much. She had Khumbu to look after, and then the second one, a boy, Linda, was born in 1968."

Jabu and Jabulani get married

After Linda's birth, Jabu went to work at Mdaphuna's, the cash store in the village. The salary was low, but Gogo Mkhize remembers how out of the little Jabu earned, she did a lot for the home.

In 1971, Jabu and Jabulani were married. The ceremony

took place at St Joseph's at Impendle and the celebration was at the Mkhize home. People came from all over the district and Jabulani invited many new friends and colleagues from Pietermaritzburg.

After their marriage, Jabulani wanted Jabu to be near him and so she left Gomane and went to live with him in Pietermaritzburg. She left Khumbu and Linda with her parents.

Phambano and Ina continued to work in the fields. But, Thoko recalls, the lands had shrunk. In the 1960s, many labour tenants were being forced to leave white farms in the area around Impendle as the government brought in laws to abolish the system of labour tenancy. Chief Zuma had to subdivide his land. Phambano's orchards and fields were ploughed up to make way for houses. Today there are only a couple of fruit trees left, and the boundary fence is close to the stoep.

In spite of these hardships, Phambano did not give up his farming. He was still ploughing two days before his death, Noma recalls.

His children remember how Phambano used to like to talk about politics. "Although the ANC was banned, he often spoke about the organisation and its leaders. If he was still alive he would have been a member," says Noma.

Phambano died on an auspicious day. People say he died with the heroes – on 16 June 1976, the day schoolchildren in Soweto rose up to protest against apartheid education. He lies buried in front of the house where his children grew up. Next to him lie two of his sons, Dumisani, who was close to Jabu, and Mzwandile. The two brothers died of illness in the 1980s.

Gogo Mkhize still has children to look after. Her

grandchildren sometimes come to stay with her and she takes in children whose parents have sent them to school in Impendle to get them away from the violence in Pietermaritzburg.

Since Jabu's death, Sanele, Jabu's youngest, has been staying with his grandmother. Gogo Mkhize speaks of his confusion and grief after the attack. "Sanele is still young, only 11. He suffered when I told him that his father had died. He cried. His uncle suggested we should take him to town to pass the house so that he would see how it had been burned. Sanele sometimes asked to see how the house had been burned. And the other daughter, Luhle, is still crying, she is crying. But they will soon forget, because they are still children."

TWO
Imbali

IMBALI, WHERE JABU AND JABULANI settled in 1972, is a township of 35 000 people about seven kilometres west of the white town of Pietermaritzburg. It is one of five townships around Pietermaritzburg, with altogether between half a million and a million people.

It is the first township on the Edendale Road, which leads out of the white suburbs to the industrial areas. If you carry on along this highway and go beyond Imbali, you travel through the giant Edendale complex, a township area made up of about 20 settlements, many of them on freehold land.

From there, you wind through the hills of the Natal Midlands and into the Vulindlela district, which is governed by KwaZulu. In Vulindlela the settlements are further apart and most of the houses are made of mud.

After you pass the tiny farming centre of Boston you turn off to Impendle. Over the years, the Ndlovu children came to know this road very well, as they often travelled to Impendle to visit their grandmother and to spend the school holidays on the farm.

Imbali is a typical apartheid township. It was built in the 1960s and 1970s at a time when the government was entrenching apartheid through pass laws, forced removals and segregation of the cities. At first Imbali was meant to house the people of Sobantu village, who were to be removed under the Group Areas Act. The Native Affairs Department said Sobantu village was too close to the white areas of Pietermaritzburg.

The residents of Sobantu village resisted being removed and, in the end, the government had to leave them alone. Sobantu would not be bulldozed. All the government could do was freeze new development in the township to force people to look for homes in other places. So when the new houses in Imbali started to become available in the 1960s, they were quickly filled up with the overflow of people from Sobantu village. Many people from Edendale were also forced to move to Imbali, although they resisted because they did not want to live in the new "matchbox" houses.

Imbali was built in "stages". Stage I, where Jabu and Jabulani lived for 16 years, was the first section to be completed. Like townships all over South Africa, Imbali has rows and rows of four-roomed houses and strict regulations to stop people building *amakoyi* – backyard shacks. But the people ignored these regulations. From the start the township was overcrowded and families needed *amakoyi* to house growing children, relatives from rural areas or newly married couples.

When Jabu and Jabulani moved to Imbali, there was already a shortage of homes in the township. All they could find was a single room in a house that they had to share with another family. But this arrangement did not work out. Jabu was pregnant with her third child, Bobo, and there was just not enough room.

So the couple moved to a house in the area of Stage I known by Imbali residents as Edamini because it is near the dam. But this accommodation was not suitable either, and shortly after Bobo, another boy, was born, they moved again. This time they were lucky enough to find and rent a four-roomed house.

A job at Prestige

Their new address was Number 373 Mthombothi Road, Stage I. They lived there for six years. But Jabu and Jabulani were also thinking of the future and put their names down on the township superintendent's waiting list to buy a house.

The family was growing and the cost of living was going up. In 1974, another daughter, Mamza, was born and Jabu realised she would have to go out and work.

So when Mamza was just three months old, Jabu applied for a job at the kitchenware factory, Prestige. She was accepted, and on 29 October 1974 Jabu started working at the job she was to keep until her death 15 years later. She became a machine operator in the press shop department. According to a friend, she would have started at about R6.30 a week. Today that would be worth only R39 a week.[13]

---

13 Update, October 2017: Inflation means that this would be about R285 today.

Prestige is an international company, with factories in other parts of South Africa and overseas. The Pietermaritzburg factory is built on a hill overlooking Imbali and the neighbouring township of Slangspruit. The factory is near Stage I. Most of the workers come from Imbali or Slangspruit and, like them, Jabu used to walk to work each day on one of the many paths leading out of the townships.

Though they are side-by-side, Imbali and Slangspruit are quite different. Slangspruit is built on freehold land which is owned by landlords who rent sites or shacks to tenants. The Pietermaritzburg town council has refused to develop the area. So Slangspruit does not have tarred roads and matchbox houses. There the people live in wattle and mud huts with corrugated iron roofs. Their homes are separated by alleys which become rivers of sludge when it rains. Many people would say Slangspruit was no more than a slum.

There are seven factories besides Prestige on the hill, which is in the industrial area the workers call KwaMeseni, after the English name, Mason's Mill. Among them are a timber factory, a brick and tile factory, a brewery and a rubber factory – and there is often the smell of hot oil and frying potatoes from the factory next door to Prestige: Simba Chips.

On the other side of Prestige, further up the hill, there used to be a furniture factory. But now it has been turned into barracks for the police and troops who patrol the townships. The policemen and soldiers hang their uniforms out to dry on the fence, and from armoured vehicles parked on top of the hill they keep watch on the townships through binoculars.

An old-fashioned factory

Like all the factories in Mason's Mill, Prestige is guarded by a high wall and a security fence. The factory looks neat and modern from the outside, but inside it is a standard old-fashioned factory. The factory floor is packed with machines and people, and the noise is deafening. The workers are mostly women, and they produce 23 000 completed kitchen utensils a day. Every day, lorries travel down the hill to Pietermaritzburg and other centres with crates of gadgets and utensils like spatulas, forks, baking tins, tongs, can openers, spoons and ladles.

In the early years at Prestige, the shifts were very much longer than the nine hours they are today. Workers sometimes spent 15 hours a day at the factory, starting at around 7:30 am. But then there was no union at Prestige, and Jabu was not involved in worker or political struggles.

Jabu's youngest sister, Bongi, recalls that she was strongly aware of how she was being exploited at Prestige. "I was still at school, and Jabu used to try and discourage me from becoming a factory worker because the life was so hard. So in the end I became a teacher," says Bongi.

After work, Jabu concentrated on her education and on her church activities. She registered with a night school to study for her matric. But the long shifts meant she had to give up her studies for the second time. A few years later she tried again for her matric, and succeeded. Jabu was not a person who gave up easily.

Like any working woman, Jabu had to deal with the pressures of work and looking after her family. She realised that she and Jabulani would need some help around the house and someone to look after the children when they were not home. Conveniently, her elder sister, Noma, was teaching at a school in Stage I and finished work in the early afternoon. Her hours meant that she would be able to look after the children in the afternoons, so Jabu asked Noma to come and live with them.

Noma was happy to accept. She had helped to look after Jabu as a child, and now she was looking after Jabu's children. "They loved me," says Noma. "Soon after Bobo was born, I was living with them, so he grew up seeing me living with them. And when Mamza was born, I was still staying with them, and when the third girl, Luhle, was born in 1977. When Bobo was still very young, one and a half, he didn't know whether Jabu was his mother or I was his mother. You know, an aunt is more lenient than a mother, and I'm sure that's why they loved me."

Family members remember the years at Mthombothi Road as being a period of great happiness. Khumbu and Linda were still with Gogo Mkhize at Impendle, and Jabulani used to visit them every weekend.

Jabulani had always wanted to be a driver, and was now working in the distribution department of the *Natal Witness*. "He was regarded as one of the best drivers," says Noma. "He was always a very active person, and fast. So if things were to be taken to the airport, he was the person who was sent, because he was the fastest driver."

"Like my own child"

Gogo Mkhize remembers Jabulani's kindness. "He was like my own child. If I was unhappy with something, he would say, 'Hey, *Mkhwekazi* [my mother-in-law] said she doesn't like that, so don't do it'. If I wanted to borrow money from him, he never complained; he just gave me the money."

Jabulani was a keen sportsman and played for the top soccer club around Pietermaritzburg – Carlton Athletics. He was known for being a fitness fanatic, and worked hard to see that "CA" stayed on top. As a coach, he warned players that if they did not work out in the gym they would not be included in the team, which defeated many opponents in the townships around Pietermaritzburg.

Jabu was not able to visit Impendle as often as her husband, but her mother always enjoyed her visits. "By then she had her own home, so she only visited during Christmas and Easter holidays, or when there was an important function. She would bring all her children, and the house became full. It was very nice – I couldn't believe that they were all my grandchildren," she says.

Noma was happy with the family, and Bongi also came to stay with them. The two sisters were still with them in 1979 when the township superintendent informed them that their names were now top of the waiting list and they could buy a house.

Noma helped Jabu and Jabulani move into their new home, at Number 437 Mkhamba Street, and it was in this house, in 1980, that Jabu had her last child, Sanele.

Until the war started, the family lived happily in Mkhamba Street. Khumbu and Linda were brought from Impendle to live at Number 437, and the house truly became the Ndlovu family home.

This is why Jabu refused to listen when her mother, fearing for their safety after the death threats began, begged her to move. This was the home Jabu tried to protect with a high security fence. And this was the home that Linda wanted to rebuild after the attack so that his brothers and sisters could be together again.

THREE

A very harmonious home

From the outside, Number 437 looked exactly like any other Imbali "matchbox". Like most homes in Imbali Stage I, it had two bedrooms, a living room, a kitchen and an outside toilet. Detached toilets are common in Imbali, and they are a feature people came to hate and fear after the war started. There were cases of people being shot going to the toilet at night.

Inside, the Ndlovu home was very special. A close friend of the family, who often stopped by, remembers Jabu's warmth and generosity. "It was like Christmas every day," she says. "They were a very harmonious home and family. You were always received with red-carpet style. Whatever was happening, you were made welcome. Jabu would tell her children, 'See who has just come in! Stop what you are doing and prepare something for her to eat!' She was very generous. And she could always make an image. Even if there had been a family dispute, you would never see it when you arrived. You would always find a

Jabu's children. From left, Bobo, Sanele, Luhle and Mamza.

peaceful family.

"The home was always immaculate and bursting with furniture. Jabu was a person with style and the husband was also like that. Jabu told me sometimes Jabulani would surprise her by just buying new furniture for the house. And she sometimes would do the same for him."

Around the house was space for a garden. Remembering what they had learned as children in Impendle, Jabu and Jabulani planted a vegetable garden and fruit trees in the back yard. In the front were the chickens. "Jabulani was very keen on the chickens," the friend remembers. "If you came there early in the morning the first thing you would see was Jabulani in his shorts feeding the chickens."

The children especially remember the chickens. According to the custom, Jabulani had given each child a chicken. "There is a Zulu saying that we can see your future through the chicks you hatch," Jabu's friend explains. "If you are given one chicken and that one chicken only rears one other small chick, and that chick rears only one small chick, it means you won't get rich – but you will make it in life. However, if your chicken rears 14 chicks, and those 14 raise 90 more, you will be rich and your riches will come easily. Life won't be a matter of the pick and shovel."

While they were living in Mkhamba Street, Jabu joined the Metal and Allied Workers Union (MAWU), which later became the National Union of Metalworkers of South Africa (NUMSA). Mamza, the eldest daughter after Khumbu, remembers Jabu as being very busy from the time she joined MAWU. "That's the first thing I can say about her," she says. "She was always very busy, every day."

Khumbu and Linda were at high school. The three younger children – Bobo, Mamza and Luhle – were attending Sgodini, a Catholic primary school in Edendale. Sanele, the baby of the family, was in Impendle with Gogo. Reluctantly, Jabu had sent him to Impendle when he was only nine months old because she could not find good childcare for the mornings.

Jabu used to get up at five in the morning to start preparing breakfast for the children. She used to leave the house at 6:30 am, winter and summer, to go to work. If she did not have union meetings, she came home at around 5:30 pm. Otherwise, the children could expect her back after 9:00 pm, often long after they had gone to bed.

At first, Mamza says, the children were jealous of the time their mother spent away from home: "In 1983 when she became a shop steward, because we were still young it was not nice for us when she went out. But as we grew up we came to accept it. We understood what the situation was like. As she was a worker, she had to fight. You see, maybe they worked too hard for too little pay, and those sorts of things. For myself, I felt it was good, although I didn't like her absence."

For Jabu, there were many meetings and seminars to attend. To help her family understand, she explained why she had joined the union and what her long absences from home were all about. She brought pamphlets home and explained that not only her own family but also the families of others would benefit through MAWU because the union was fighting for better wages and working conditions.

She also told her family that now that she was a union member as well as a worker, everybody would have to share household tasks. So together the family worked out ways of sharing housework so that Jabu would be free to take up the struggles at Prestige.

Noma and Khumbu were very important to the household. Khumbu was 16 years old when Jabu joined MAWU. She was already used to looking after her younger sisters and brothers and, with Noma, helping them with their homework.

During the week, Noma or Khumbu used to prepare food. But in Jabu's house, there were no rules for what boys should do or what girls should do. Jabu's sons also had to learn their way around the kitchen, so when Khumbu was away visiting Impendle or staying with friends, Linda had to take over her cooking duties.

Linda had a good example in his father. Jabulani also used to like cooking and often helped with the housework. "What I used to like most about my father was that he liked to cook," says Mamza. "His special food was hot curry. And he used to be responsible and help us as we cleaned up."

Each of the children had little jobs around the house, Mamza remembers, and they all helped each other. "Linda used to be the one for the front garden. He didn't like the back yard because it was so stony and hard to clean. So my father used to do that, and my mother used to plant vegetables and herbs, or tell them what they should plant. Linda also had to clean the kitchen. Bobo would have to clean the bedroom. And I had to clean the dining room. Luhle would have to do the toilet or, because she was younger, just pick up papers around the yard."

Getting the boys to do certain tasks was sometimes an uphill battle. "Linda never used to like cleaning the stoep," says Mamza. "He used to say, 'Mamza, just imagine me kneeling there, with people looking at me'."

But Jabu's teaching paid off. Years later, after her death, when Linda's friends used to nag him about cleaning or washing up, he used to do it. "But he used to tell them, 'You sound just like my mother!'" Mamza remembers.

Jabu was luckier than many other women workers. Many husbands refused to allow their wives to go to union meetings for fear they were meeting other men there, or would neglect their homes. But Luhle remembers how her father used to joke about Jabu's union and political activities.

"He was just fine, but he used to ask: 'Do all the other women go out like you, at night, and stay out late?' But he was just joking, and my mother just used to laugh."

At weekends, if there were no meetings, the family would be together. But often Jabu was tired and it was Jabulani who spent time with the children: "I remember how we used to dance on Friday and Saturday nights," says Luhle. "Maybe we wouldn't go to sleep. And my mother sometimes used to shout at us, 'It's night! You are making a noise!' But we just kept quiet for a few minutes, and when she was asleep we would start again."

Every Sunday, if she were not committed to union or community meetings, Jabu would go to the Catholic church in Mthombothi Road with her children. Afterwards they would have Sunday lunch together, "like a family," says Mamza.

FOUR
MAWU comes to Prestige

THERE ARE 150 FULL-TIME WORKERS at Prestige. Of these, about 120 are women. There are six departments on the factory floor, producing 448 different kinds of kitchen utensils.

In the industrial bakeware department, workers make bread and cake tins for the big bakeries. In the plastics and assembly department, workers make plastic handles and attach them to kitchen utensils. In the plating department, workers paint utensils and coat them with chrome. Then there is the warehouse, and Jabu's department, the press shop.

One of the bosses described the press shop as "a very masculine environment" – yet most of the 55 people who work there are women. There are two kinds of presses – small presses and big presses. You need plenty of strength and muscle to operate the presses.

The work is laborious and monotonous. It is hot and noisy. All day long there is the sound of clanging and tearing as the small presses cut sheets of metal into utensils like spoons or graters. It is even worse where the big presses are: here giant machines lift and drop weights of up to 150 tons onto metal sheets to crush and bend them into different sizes and shapes of bakeware and other products. Jabu worked both kinds of presses. When she died, she was working on the big presses. She was earning about R180 a week.

In the press shop, the workers have earplugs and gloves, safety measures Jabu fought for when she was a shop steward. The workers are still fighting to have fans installed to deal with the heat.

In 1974, when Jabu started working at Prestige, there was no union in the factory. A close friend and union comrade, who started working at Prestige a few years before Jabu, remembers their long hours and bad working conditions: "The women started at 7:30 am and knocked off at 10:30 pm. You won't believe it, but at that time we were earning R6.30 a week. We had to be thankful for what the employer was giving us."

There was racism in the factory: African workers were never chosen for certain jobs, which were reserved for whites. Workers could be dismissed without explanation.

Overtime was not fairly paid and workers were not given uniforms or overalls. Health and safety regulations either did not exist or were ignored. Sometimes, workers who became pregnant would lose their jobs when they went home to have their babies.

"Many grievances but no voice"

Workers got increases on "so-called merit", the friend remembers. "When the boss liked you, he gave you an increase. But when he did not like you, no matter how hard you worked, he did not give you an increase."

Workers at Prestige had many grievances but no voice, says Jabu's friend. "We were not happy but could not complain because if we did we were threatened with dismissal. That is why, when the union started, we decided to join."

The two MAWU organisers who first came to the factory gates with pamphlets in 1981 were Geoff Schreiner and John Makhathini. Management immediately called a meeting of workers to remind them that they had a liaison committee.

Liaison committees were the creation of management in terms of legislation aimed at preventing African workers from forming independent unions. Workers would choose half the members of the liaison committees and the bosses would choose the other half.

Management encouraged workers in their factories to support liaison committees instead of unions, because the committees made it easier to control workers and prevent strikes. But workers saw liaison committees as toothless bodies.

In the early 1980s, the position of African workers all over the country was like that of the workers at Prestige. Workers were not well organised. Thousands had no union at all, although the trade union movement was growing again as a result of a wave of wage strikes which began in Durban in 1973.

Twenty years before the Durban strikes, in the 1950s, the South African Congress of Trade Unions (SACTU) had tried to organise workers under the banner of non-racialism. But fearing a united working class and because of SACTU's links with the African National Congress (ANC), the state had crushed SACTU by banning and jailing its leaders. By 1965, SACTU was no longer operating in South Africa. Those leaders who had not been banned or jailed went into exile. The non-racial trade union movement had been smashed.

The Bantu Labour Act

The government introduced new laws aimed at discouraging Africans from forming unions. One of these laws was the Bantu Labour Act. It was this law which created the system of "liaison committees", aimed at replacing unions in the factories.

The Durban strikes of the early 1970s broke the silence caused by the repression of the 1950s and 1960s. Rising prices were biting into workers' pockets, and more than 60 000 workers from 146 different factories took part in the strikes. After the strikes, workers began to organise again to build strong unions. Jabu's union, MAWU, was one of the unions born out of this strike.

MAWU held its first meeting in May 1973 in Edendale, outside Pietermaritzburg, and from there began organising in factories all over the country. Slowly its numbers grew, and soon MAWU members in factories throughout South Africa were pushing for recognition agreements.

Jabu joined MAWU in 1981. In 1983 she became a shop

steward, and in 1985 she took over as senior shop steward. Many workers remember how she fought with them for recognition at Prestige.

FIVE

We want to join!

IN 1988 JABU WENT OVERSEAS. We shall hear more about her travels later, but while she was overseas she was interviewed by members of an American video team, the Labour Video Unit. She told them why she joined MAWU and about the long struggle for recognition at Prestige. This is what she said:

* * *

Geoff Schreiner and John Makhathini came to distribute pamphlets at the factory gate. Because I was then very blind, I didn't know there was something that was called a union. Then everyone, all of us in the factory, we used to just grab the papers to please them. Grab the paper and look at it, then just drop it down in front of them.

They would come daily, until we started complaining, "Hęy, why are you always wanting us? We are tired, man, we have been working. What are these papers for?" Then they said, "Oh, could you please just read, grab the paper and read it." But we still grabbed them and dropped them.

Then there were some people who told us, "Look, there is something which is called a union. It does this, it does that, but you must join it first." Then after some time, we said, "No, we must have a meeting one day."

John Makhathini came, and at a meeting in a certain church, he explained more about the union. Then we said, "Now. Now, before we leave, we want to join." Then we joined.

John Makhathini told us the structures, that if you join the union, there must be an election of shop stewards according to departments. We elected about ten shop stewards.

But after that, we had a problem, because even if the horses are pulling, they don't pull exactly the same. There are those lazy horses which need the sjambok. Some of them were too lazy to attend meetings.

The following year we decided to elect half the number. Then everything went well. We were trying to push left and right. But we had a serious problem when the management were asking, "Why did you join the union?" They were calling us into their offices just for that, twice a day, every day.

The management were trying to pressurise us from the beginning to be scared of carrying on with the union, because we didn't have a recognition agreement at that time. But we were going to push for an agreement.

We told the boss that we wanted our rights: "In this factory there are so many dismissals, daily dismissals. We are sick and tired of those things. And there are no proper working facilities. We want everything to be improved."

"Look at our hands!"

He said, "I am paying you a lot of money." We said, "A lot of money can't look after my life. I need things which will look after my life. Look at our hands!" Our hands were full of scratches. There was a sharp material which was used there, without gloves.

He said, "No, I will NEVER sign an agreement!" Then we went for a caucus. In the following meeting with us, he said, "I will NEVER..." We said, "You will. You will sign an agreement. Or you can improve everything 100 per cent, then we'll forget about the union. You can improve everything: wages, conditions, your first aid, your canteen, your toilets, your machines as well. Any machine which has hurt a person you must be prepared to do something about. Otherwise, you will sign an agreement."

He said, "I am an international company. I can't sign an agreement. I have got some people who are superior to me." Then we said, "It's very good if you've got your superiors. Let them come to the meeting. You leave the meeting to them. You go out, because you can do nothing. Admit that you are a worker, like ourselves." It went on till the twelfth month; then he said, "There are some people in Britain..." We said, "Phone them now, tell them that we have been patient enough. Now we want an agreement."

He said, "No, I can't." We said, "Today we want one thing: an answer, yes or no. Are you prepared to sign or not?" He said, "Eh, I've got this ... I've got problems ... Eh, I haven't got enough money. I've got..."

"Are you prepared to sign or not? Tell us. Yes or no. Then we'll go back and tell the shop floor."

Then he said, "Oh, let me phone the people in Britain and ask them." He went up to the office. Geoff Schreiner said, "Just follow him and see whether he phones or not. Maybe he is just standing in the kitchen there." Then the management phoned us and said there was a Mr Fox, who was from overseas.

Then we said, "As soon as this gentleman from overseas arrives, we want to talk to him." Then they asked, "What are you going to tell him?" We said, "We want an agreement on the many things that we have been telling you about. Unfair dismissals and the machines. As a boss, these are his machines. People have got six fingers, eight fingers because of these *skorokoros* [wrecks] in this factory. We are sick and tired of them."

Then, when Mr Fox came, they said, "Oh, he has arrived." They said he is going to spend a week. His first day was the Monday morning. Then on Thursday we said, "Hey, tomorrow is the last day; we want to see the gentleman!"

They said, "Oh, this gentleman has gone."

"Why?" we said.

They said, "Oh, never mind, he has given us the right to sign an agreement."

We said, "Okay, sign."

And he started to jib, 'Oh, I meant so and so…"

We said, "No, we are sick and tired of excuses. You can't be making excuses for 12 months."

Then he said, "Oh no, I am going to sign. Here is a piece of paper."

It was just a draft of an agreement. We signed, and then we said that if he starts to jib again, then we are going to take him to court. Then he signed the agreement. We said, "We don't want a preliminary agreement." So we have a full agreement now. Signed.

SIX
I used to be just a quiet person

Jabu told the Labour Video Unit how joining the union changed her life:

* * *

I used to be just a quiet person, really, but I could get cross quickly. My mother used to say that I was a cheeky person when I was young. At the factory, I used to keep quiet. But not since I joined the union.

I saw how the workers are working, the supervisors pushing, so that you are sweating. The factory is very hot. No one is looking after the workers. The heat makes you sick. You become dizzy; you get a severe headache; you have heart problems when you are working in a very, very hot place for a long time.

The workers didn't fight. Instead the supervisor kept

on pushing us. And then in the afternoon he dismissed two people. On the following day, he dismissed three. When it came to Christmas, he dismissed 15, whoever he likes – the supervisor, not even the boss.

Then, when we had the first meeting, seeing that I was so cross, the workers said, "Hey, you must be a shop steward!" Then because I was so cross I said, "Let me take this thing." I wasn't clear about the struggle then, but because I wanted to tell the boss something I agreed … I agreed.

Then when I started to attend meetings I had to learn many things from other shop stewards – people who were shop stewards before, like the Sarmcol workers.

Phineas, the one who died. That was a strong man. He used to keep quiet, but when he was talking he used to give you something. So I gradually picked up by being active, attending union meetings, attending community meetings. I had to learn many things on my own.

We started working on women's problems when we joined the union. We said equal pay for equal jobs, because we saw we were working on the same machines, were working the same hours. So there was no reason for the bosses to say that we should get a lower wage.

The company was not against that. They didn't give us any problem – they said that they are prepared to give us equal pay. But in the union we have the problem that some people are still very weak. They are afraid to express themselves, saying that as women we must get this, though we are with men.

Like maternity leave. We have just improved it from three months to six months. Babies sometimes die because they do not have good care from their mothers, are left after one month with someone who might not look after them well. The problem is that the maternity leave is unpaid. But we are trying to fight for a few rands from the sick pay fund. And we can apply for some money from the unemployment fund. But to start off with, no one has done this because people are hesitant: "Oh, if I am the one who is going to start this thing, then I am afraid." They are still weak.

"It must be fifty-fifty."

Now we are trying to have meetings to educate people that there is no difference between a man and a woman. It is fifty-fifty. Whether you are married or not, it must be fifty-fifty.

How can we say that people shall share, when we are not sharing at home? We must share everything at home: work, looking after babies, paying accounts, paying for the rent.

What happens is this – when a man says, "Oh, here is the money", he forgets one thing – that this money won't run to the office and pay the rent. It won't run to the shop and pay the account. We must get his help. If I am working on a Saturday, he must go out and pay accounts.

But the men are so staunch. They have a custom which says once you cook at home, it means you have been defeated by the wife. There is a Zulu custom saying a man mustn't do anything. He must just sit and relax, waiting for the food. He waits for the wife to do the washing.

You give birth – six children, eight children – no one is helping you. Now those customs were for ancient people where women were not working and the fathers used to plough in the fields. They looked after our cattle then. I, as a woman, I'd stay at home and do the washing. I'd do the cooking. Now there is no time for that because I am also working like him. We wake up early in the morning, myself and him, and there is no one at home during the day. So he must know that as soon as he arrives home he must start and do something in the kitchen for me. Then I must come and help him. Wipe this clean; I must bath the babies … We must share everything. Then we can say that people shall share.

* * *

SEVEN
Comrade and friend

MANY OF JABU'S COMRADES REMEMBER her strength and her commitment to the struggle. John Makhathini remembers the impression Jabu made on him at the first meeting the MAWU organisers called at the Presbyterian Church in Imbali.

"The aim of the meeting was to explain to Prestige workers what is MAWU and what is a union. I explained that they would have to elect shop stewards. I stressed that we needed strong workers in the company because it's not an easy job to be a shop steward. It's not myself as organiser who is a union, it is the workers themselves."

Right from the early days, while Jabu was vice-chair at Prestige, Makhathini would see her at every meeting. "During that time, I think she was wanting to learn about trade unions. She was careful to understand exactly the job of a shop steward. We often called mass general meetings and local general meetings, and she came to all those meetings. She was very active, from the start, not only at the later stage when she died. She was very strong from the beginning. She was not scared; she would push left and right until she got what she wanted from the company. And in our structures, if she believed the point was right, she would push it. I watched her growing as a leader."

Jabu was a good tactician and strategist. "I think she used to study management before wage negotiations," says Makhathini. "She was using a lot of tactics, you see. She did not only have one style – she was pushing hardline and softline. You could see the manager, Mr Snowdon, used to turn red and white when she was using a hardline. You would hear Mr Snowdon cry – 'Ai, Jabu, wait!' – but she would push her point. I used to be there sometimes, but involved with Jabu in caucus. She used to say, 'Makhathini, keep quiet. I will deal with the management. Don't say anything.' Sometimes the company would run to me to find out my position. Maybe they saw I would be softer than Jabu. Jabu understood the managers – each manager."

A shop steward remembers the tricks and strategies she and Jabu used at the negotiation table. "We had a way of telling each other when to speak and when to stop. She knew that when I touched her with my foot, she must put a full stop so that I could start speaking. We always removed our shoes so that we would be able to touch each other with our toenails."

There were many strikes and stayaways during Jabu's time. "Most of the strikes we won," the shop steward recalls, "because we did not strike for a minor thing. We stopped work only for important things."

"The bosses called the police."

"Once we went on strike because they had fired a woman who was a shop steward. We were in the hall. The bosses called the police. It was the first time that they called the police for a strike. Even then they failed.

"We asked the police if the employer had told them that in our recognition agreement we had 24 hours' wildcat strike time. We were not breaking any agreement. So after that they took out the workers who are *amagundane* – who are rats – who do not belong to any union, telling them we were going to be beaten by Boers with sjamboks.

"But the Boers went away with their sjamboks. We went out without being beaten. We were not forced out by the employer."

After she became a senior shop steward at Prestige, Jabu taught what she had struggled to learn in the beginning to new shop stewards. One comrade, who became a shop steward in 1988, told how Jabu gave her courage.

"Jabu was the one who was pushing me. I did not like to stand. She taught me that she did not easily become what she was – she had to be really strong.

"At the factory she was brave. She would just tell a person if she was wrong, not gossip about her. She confronted people. I saw her as a person who had good advice. At the factory, when we were still new, we knew she was there and was going to push.

"When we were sitting down with management, she apportioned points so that one of us would say this, and another that. She did not want it to be only her who was talking. She wanted us to participate, to get experience."

"She had a lot of tricks."

Another close friend and union comrade, who became a shop steward in the early days after the recognition agreement was signed, says: "I started learning bit by bit, with Jabu encouraging me. She told me I should go to meetings and speak at meetings – not necessarily because I was a shop steward, but to practise for negotiations.

"Jabu taught me the techniques of being a shop steward, techniques of negotiating, techniques of seating at meetings. She taught me how a shop steward should behave. If it were not for her, I would not be like this.

"She also had a lot of tricks. Say, for example, the management was harassing the workers, what should we do? We should have a secret caucus – and we would have that in the toilets. After planning with her in the toilet we would go and consult with the supervisor.

"And when I had problems in my family, I told Jabu and she would advise me. Say, for instance, we were supposed to go to a seminar, so we would not go back home. My husband would say no, you are not going. Who is going to be doing the cooking? Jabu gave me techniques – "You must talk, you must tell him this and that." – for convincing my husband.

"Right from the start she was a very, very strong woman. From the word go until the very end. I'm very proud of what I am now, and it's because of Jabu."

In South Africa – as in other places – it is difficult for women to become shop stewards. There are many reasons for this. Often women workers lack confidence because of their oppression, and so will not stand for leadership positions. Sometimes male workers oppose women when they stand for election. Sometimes their husbands won't allow them to stand. Most women carry the burdens of childcare and housework and feel they do not have the time or energy to take on a shop steward's duties. In some factories, even women workers are reluctant to vote other women into office, because they lack confidence in women office bearers.

In Jabu's time at Prestige, there were four women shop stewards and one man, and right from the start the senior shop stewards were women. "There were never any complaints from the men at Prestige about being led by women," says one of the male shop stewards. "The men treated them as their sisters."

"Men's issues"

"But there were some exceptional issues that were secret which had to be addressed by males in private," he says. "For example, if we needed to talk about the love affairs of a man. Such issues had to be dealt with privately. Women comrades might take it further, because they might understand these affairs as exploitation of other women."

A comrade who started working at Prestige in 1980 says, "Jabu was bold! Whether you were a supervisor, or whether you were a manager, or whether you were a director, she would confront you. She would drive her point home. And if the management did not understand, she would repeat herself until they did.

"I remember one incident where we took action for awards. For long service, the company used to give us badges somehow designed so that when you worked for ten years, they would write 'Ten Years' on them. But we didn't benefit, because they were only paper. So we demanded that the company must give us something worth money. We took action. During that action the management decided to face us and Jabu stood up and said, 'Give the people what they want. They want proper awards, not these paper awards that you are designing.' The company eventually gave us money awards. So now we get proper pay for long service, calculated for each year."

Another friend remembers a similar battle: "There was a sort of necklace that you would get after ten years. And Jabu said, 'No, this is nothing! Give the people something!' So they gave them wristwatches."

Towards the middle of the 1980s, women's voices were beginning to be heard in the unions. Women workers were demanding a firmer stand on issues like maternity benefits and childcare. Jabu and a close comrade attended many seminars on women's issues and joined debates within the unions about whether women workers should organise separately. Later, Jabu joined the NUMSA Women's Forum, which made sure that campaigns around women's health, childcare and maternity pay were taken up.

Eventually, the war started to make inroads into Jabu's time, and the Women's Forum was finding it difficult to organise in Pietermaritzburg. But in Jabu's time the women of NUMSA won important victories in the factories and in the unions. Women's campaigns are still important today, and Jabu's name often comes up in discussions around women's issues.

Another project that was especially close to Jabu's heart was the Prestige Choir. Jabu and another shop steward together decided to form the choir to help organise the women. Patty Henderson, a cultural worker, remembers how the choir used to practise at the factory at lunchtimes.

"I used to bring drums and instruments to the factory," she says. "We didn't have much time to practise – only about 15 minutes. But the spirit was very good."

The Prestige Choir came to be well known in Imbali. As the years went by, the choir sang at many rallies and cultural events. There was a time in the war, the Comrades say, when all other organisations had been smashed in Imbali. But if there was a rally, you could always depend on Jabu and the Prestige Choir to be there.

EIGHT
The year the war began

PEOPLE IN IMBALI SAY THE WAR started in 1985. The first serious attacks came that year. Before then, the Comrades say, there wasn't an Inkatha problem; there was just a police problem.

The war started after the formation of the United Democratic Front (UDF) in 1983. The government had announced a "new deal" for South Africa. They were going to introduce a tricameral parliament. Whites, coloureds and Indians would be represented, but Africans would be left out. The UDF united civics, youth, students', women's and church organisations to fight against the "new deal".

The UDF was popular. New organisations were springing up in the townships to fight the new parliamentary system as well as the system of community councils, and these organisations quickly affiliated to the UDF. The community councils were new town councils for African townships. But people all over the country realised that the community councils would have very little power and refused to support them.

The people's fears were confirmed when the government made it clear that it would no longer provide money for facilities in the townships, so the community councils would have to raise their own finances. To solve the problem, the councils put up rents. But in Imbali, as in other townships, workers earned low wages and many people were unemployed. The new rents would bring great suffering. Anger against the councils increased.

During this period, new organisations were being formed in Imbali. In 1983, the Congress of South African Students (COSAS) was organising in schools in Imbali. Youth who were not students started to join the Imbali Youth Organisation (IYO). Both these organisations were affiliated to the UDF. In 1985, Imbali residents formed the Imbali Civic Association (ICA) to oppose the Imbali Community Council.

Workers were also consolidating their power. The Congress of South African Trade Unions (COSATU) was launched in November 1985. It was the biggest union federation ever in South Africa, with 33 affiliates and 500 000 members. Jabu's union, MAWU, was a founder member of COSATU.

From the start, COSATU resolved not to separate political and worker struggles. Because of this, Inkatha, the political party of KwaZulu, saw the UDF and COSATU as threats to its power in Natal.

Soon after COSATU was launched, the Inkatha leader, Chief Mangosuthu Buthelezi, announced that he was considering forming his own trade union federation to challenge COSATU. He said COSATU was hostile to Inkatha. In May 1986, the Inkatha union, the United

Workers Union of South Africa (UWUSA) was launched at a rally in Durban and started organising in Natal.

It was around this time that Jabu was approached by a senior Inkatha official to spy on MAWU. An organiser remembers how she proved her loyalty to her union and her comrades.

Jabu is asked to spy

"Jabu was a very loyal friend. I say this because she told me one night a high official of KwaZulu came to her house to ask her to work for him. I think it was because Gatsha would be very grateful to get information about MAWU – what we are doing, what we are saying about Gatsha Buthelezi. She refused to work for him. She refused to give information about our unions. After that the relationship between Jabu and the Zulu MP was not good."

The people of Imbali got their first taste of teargas and birdshot in 1984 when the Minister of Cooperation and Development, Piet Koornhof, visited Imbali. Koornhof had been appearing on platforms all over the country. You would often see him on TV, dressed in zebra skins, inaugurating community councils and conferring powers on community council chairmen.

The president of the Imbali Youth Organisation, Skhumbuzo Ngwenya, remembers the anger that exploded when Imbali's turn for a Koornhof visit came. "Until then, Imbali people only knew political upheavals as something they saw on TV, happening in other areas. The first victim of our struggle in Imbali died on the day of Piet Koornhof's visit. He was Muzi Ntombela, shot by a security policeman.

He was not even an active member of the IYO – he was just a schoolboy."

Linda's problems begin

Even after 16 June 1976, when students all over South Africa followed the lead of their comrades in Soweto to rise up against "gutter" education, Natal was peaceful. Skhumbuzo was in Standard 8 [Grade 10] in 1976. "I wasn't really involved in politics at that time, but I read about the violence in the newspapers. Here in Maritzburg it wasn't severe. We sympathised with the students against the police. But we did not say whether what the kids were doing was right or wrong. And there was no political organisation of the students to take up the issues of '76. Inkatha mobilised itself against the IYO and the civics in 1985. That's when they started burning houses, and that's when they started attacking COSAS members and SRC members in schools. In 1985 we lost quite a number of our activists."

Linda had to flee school in 1985. He was studying at Siyahlomula High School at Ashdown and he had been elected an SRC member and was an active member of COSAS. So when Inkatha youth began raiding schools, he was one of their targets.

"That's when his problems began," says his cousin, who was also a student. "He used to tell me, '*Mzala* [cousin], we left school at nine or ten in the morning. The Inkatha people came to attack us at school.' At times he used to say somebody had told him that there were people looking for him. I wanted to know why this was happening. He told me it was because he was chosen as a member of the SRC.

"From that time, his family used to fear for his life. His mother even decided she wanted to go to the principal of the school to find out if he was aware what was going on, and that her son was being attacked. At times he used to flee on foot from Ashdown to Imbali – that's far, about an hour's walk for a grown man."

After being chased out of school, Linda joined the IYO. In 1985 the IYO was fighting against evictions. People had received letters warning them to demolish shacks they had built in their yards and evict the tenants – even if those tenants were members of their own families.

Skhumbuzo remembers that struggle: "In four rooms you can't accommodate all the members of the family. The young men and women were the victims of the housing crisis and so they were the people who used to build *amakoyi*. The township management had stopped developing Imbali. Therefore, we felt it was unfair of the superintendent to say we must demolish our shack houses.

"Another issue was the fighting between UDF youth and Black Consciousness youth that was going on in Imbali. For instance, Unit 13 was fighting Stage I, and Slangspruit was fighting Stage II. We had to organise the youth to regard one another as brothers and sisters rather than as enemies."

A direct challenge

In July 1985 the leader of the Imbali Civic Association, Robert Duma, had his house petrol bombed. He had to flee. Skhumbuzo explains why the ICA came under attack: "The ICA was taking up issues head on against the authorities. By challenging evictions and rents, for example, the ICA was challenging the community councillors, because they were the people who were evicting residents. By challenging the community councillors, you were seen to be challenging Inkatha, because all the old councillors are Inkatha members. And whoever challenges them, challenges the KwaZulu government because Inkatha is the KwaZulu government's organisation. I think that's when Inkatha felt the threat. Before, IYO was challenging the township superintendent about demolishing shacks. But ICA was directly challenging the community councillors."

So from around 1985 onwards, there was confusion and fear in the township. Community and youth organisations were under constant surveillance and attack.

At the same time, the onslaught against COSATU unions was beginning. MAWU found itself in the frontline of the violence. The issue that sparked the violence against MAWU members was the Sarmcol strike.

NINE
The Sarmcol strike

IN APRIL 1985, 950 WORKERS at the BTR Sarmcol factory at Howick, about 20 kilometres away from Pietermaritzburg, went on strike. The company had refused to recognise their union, MAWU. A few days later, on May 2, BTR Sarmcol dismissed all those who had downed tools. MAWU immediately launched a national solidarity campaign calling for their reinstatement.

Most of the workers came from Mpophomeni, a small township not far from Howick. Mpophomeni is just like Imbali, with rows and rows of four-roomed houses. Many of the workers also came from Impendle, where Jabu was born.

The sacking of the 950 workers caused great suffering in Mpophomeni. Many families had no money coming in. They tried to fight the company through the courts, and when that failed they boycotted shops in Howick. Workers in Durban and Johannesburg demonstrated and went on solidarity strikes.

In June, workers demonstrated in Pietermaritzburg and in the Ecumenical Lay Centre in Edendale. There was a protest march through Imbali. In July, there was a mass stayaway by workers around Pietermaritzburg. In August, as BTR continued to operate using scab labour, Pietermaritzburg workers followed the lead of Sarmcol workers, and started a boycott of white-owned shops.

Sarmcol still refused to negotiate or to refer the dispute to the Industrial Court. Their children were starving, and the Mpophomeni workers set up the Sarmcol Workers Health Committee to look into malnutrition and illness caused by the strike.

To keep their spirits up, the workers involved themselves in cultural activities. They created a play, *The Long March*, which toured the country to mobilise support for their cause.

Jabu was among a group of MAWU members from Pietermaritzburg who went to Howick to show solidarity with the BTR Sarmcol workers. Workers at Prestige also donated money for their families.

Then, in December 1986, 19 months after the sacking, Mpophomeni was attacked by members of Inkatha and UWUSA. Residents say an *impi* arrived on that day and took over the community centre. Some members of the *impi* left the hall and went into the community. They kidnapped four people and assaulted them.

Later that night, they drove off with the four in their car. Three of the people were found dead in the car the next day. They had been shot and burned to death. They were Phineas Sibiya, chairman of the BTR Sarmcol shop stewards committee, Filomena Mnikathi, an active voluntary worker for the health committee, and Simon

Ngubane, a shop steward and a cultural worker, who took part in *The Long March*. The fourth person, Micca Sibiya, Phineas's brother, managed to escape by jumping out of the car and rolling down a cliff. He heard the shots being fired during the night.

The morning after the attack, the *impi* left the community centre and invaded the township, and another young man was killed. The attack was clearly directed against MAWU — nearly all MAWU shop stewards' houses were visited.

More than three years later, an inquest magistrate found that nine Inkatha members, including the assistant national organiser of the Inkatha Youth Brigade, Joseph Mabaso, were responsible for the killings. Today, four years later, still no one has been prosecuted.

Jabu is threatened with death

The murders shocked workers throughout the country. Local and international campaigns around the Sarmcol strike intensified. BTR Sarmcol became known as "Blood Tears and Repression".

There were also other issues which brought attacks against MAWU members. Towards the end of 1986, Jabu was threatened with death. Workers say that the first death threat came as a result of the Moses Mayekiso campaign. This campaign had begun after Moses Mayekiso, a MAWU organiser, was detained. Comrade Moss, as he was known, was picked up as he arrived back in Johannesburg from a union trip to Sweden. With four of his comrades, he was later charged with treason.

To protest against the detentions, MAWU organised one-day work stoppages at different factories, and demonstrations. Prestige workers supported this action.

"There was a time when we went out during lunch. We went out of the gate shouting *Amandla!* Everyone came out, also from the other factories, puzzled. We were saying that Mayekiso was our brother in the struggle, showing that we were not happy, as he was locked up without even knowing why. In most of the campaigns Prestige showed concern, like the Mayekiso campaign and the Sarmcol campaign," a worker remembers.

But not all Prestige workers welcomed the "Viva Moss" protests. Some workers' husbands, who were Inkatha supporters, heard about the demonstrations and tried to put a stop to them. Another worker takes up the story:

"The day after the demonstrations outside the factory – where we were wearing our "Moss" T-shirts – four people, workers' husbands, came to the gate. They said they were going to kill us, kill all the people belonging to the union because of the demonstrations. With our union officials we decided to see lawyers to try and get an interdict. Jabu also said that there was a car that was following her, harassing her, looking for her.

"It didn't bother Jabu. She said she wouldn't be leaving the union because of these people. But her husband was sensitive and said she should stop going to meetings in the afternoon. But later, when it quietened down, she carried on coming to meetings. She was a very brave woman."

The workers fought back through the courts and they won an interdict against an Imbali warlord, Michael Thu Ngcobo, to restrain him from harassing Prestige workers.

About two years later, on 24 April 1989 – just less than

a month before the attack on Jabu's house – Comrade Moss and his fellow treason trialists were acquitted and released from prison.

TEN
We are crying in Maritzburg

BY THE END OF 1987, JABU'S FAMILY was beginning to suffer the strains of the war as both Jabu and Linda came under pressure.

Jabu was getting "funny phone calls", and Jabulani feared for her life. Mysterious callers would ring the house at odd times. At the other end would be voices warning that the house was being watched. Or the phone would ring and there would be no one at the other end – as if the callers just wanted to know who was home, says Noma.

Many homes in Imbali had been attacked, and the people inside killed, whether they were involved in the struggle or not. It was becoming clear that the most vulnerable people were those who were at home most of the time – the women and children.

Jabulani and Jabu both worked during the day. By now Jabulani was working at a brewery in Pietermaritzburg. He had joined the Food and Allied Workers Union (FAWU), but was not as active as Jabu, who was often out at meetings at night.

So in Jabu's family it was Khumbu, who was unemployed and looking for a place at a teachers' training college, and Luhle, who was still going to school in Pietermaritzburg, who were mostly at home. Jabu had sent Bobo and Mamza away to school at Msinga because of the violence in the schools, and Noma had moved out of the house to go and stay with her youngest brother, Temba.

Linda was never at home. Like other Comrades, he was in hiding almost all the time. He came home only to fetch food, clothing or money.

Noma recalls how, at times, Jabu and Jabulani used to argue about Linda's political involvement. Fearing for his safety, Jabulani wanted Linda to withdraw from the youth organisation, but Jabu always replied that Linda's politics were his own choice and that only he could decide about his future. These arguments eventually won Jabulani over.

"When Linda came home, I would see Jabulani welcoming his son," says Noma. "I remember at one time when Linda came, Jabu wasn't there. Jabulani said, 'Khumbu, just forget about making me food. Just make Linda some food quickly, because after ten minutes these people who are after him will be here.'"

Tension and fear at Number 437

"I said, 'How will they know he is here?' He said, 'No, we've got a feeling that there are some informers around our place, because each time Linda comes here, ten minutes or 15 minutes after he has left, the police or the blues [*kitskonstabels* – policemen with very basic training][14] come'. And he used to give Linda money because he couldn't stay long at home."

Linda remained strong. Noma says Jabu never pushed him in any direction: "He made his own choices politically. But he and Jabu seemed to have similar brains ... They had something similar in mind."

There was now tension and fear in the Ndlovu family home. Number 437 Mkhamba Street started to become a focus of vigilante attention and police raids.

There were often sleepless nights for the family. Noma would visit Jabu in the mornings, and Jabu would tell her how they had been woken by police looking for Linda and other boys. "I remember one December holiday, I had to take Linda and Bobo to Impendle so that they could at least stay peacefully for a while.

"All the children were worried about what was going on. Mamza's schoolwork started suffering. She used to write and tell me that she couldn't study – she was always thinking about home, about Linda and her mother. She was completely disturbed by this problem.

"There was a time when even I couldn't do my schoolwork properly. Linda was being followed all the time. Jabu used to send a child to me at school to call me. She would tell me about the threats and the raids.

"After she was threatened at Prestige, our brother Temba used to borrow Jabulani's car to take her to work in the mornings and fetch her in the afternoons because it

---

14 Update, October 2017: See footnote 12 in the Introduction to the second edition for more information on *kitskonstabels*.

wasn't safe for her to walk, she would be killed. She had been told there would be someone lying in waiting for her."

There was danger everywhere. Jabu told a friend about an incident at a taxi rank. One Saturday, while she was out shopping, a well-known warlord in Imbali tried to force her into his Kombi. She knew that this meant death or assault, and refused, telling the warlord if she was going to die, it would be in her own home. "She said she wasn't fighting with any individual. She was fighting apartheid and oppression," her friend remembers.

Over the months, the warlords' reign of terror got worse. The people of Imbali felt defenceless. They believed the police were on the side of the warlords and Inkatha and would do nothing to protect them. So to defend their community and themselves, the youth organised themselves into defence teams.

Linda joins a defence team

Members of these defence teams would guard different areas of Imbali day and night. Look-outs would give the alarm if they saw anything strange – like a car circling or groups of strangers loitering. When an area was attacked, the defence teams would call sympathetic people from outside Imbali, from the white areas, to come and see what was happening – lawyers, or priests, or members of progressive organisations. If necessary, the youth would fight. Linda became a member of a defence team.

Jabu's favourite song in this period, when she led the singing at May Day and other rallies, was *Siyakhala eMgungundlovu* – "We are crying in Maritzburg". Friends of Jabu's, who also lived in Stage I, spoke about their suffering as a result of the war. They understood why this was Jabu's song.

"From 1985, the government forces, the Security Forces – policemen, *kitskonstabels*, all those elements of the government – were beating, crushing the people in the township. Some people were beaten to death – that is why we sing that we are crying. At night, we heard people screaming because 'the system' was there, harassing people, taking people secretly to jail.

"Sometimes a person was taken because he was going to die – so that now no one knows where he is, or where she is. And after some time we find out that there has been a death. You don't know who has died or who has done the killing. That is why we are crying in Pietermaritzburg. From 1985 until now, people are crying. We are still dying the same deaths as people who died in 1985."

Through all this, Jabu continued to fight. She argued that it was not enough only to be involved in workers' struggles. She said workers were also part of the community and should therefore help build community organisations. But the task was not easy. Organisations like the ICA and the IYO had been crushed or driven underground. And there was no strong women's organisation.

The birth of NUMSA

During this period, the IYO saw the women of Prestige, under Jabu's leadership, as the backbone of the struggle in Imbali. Following the COSATU policy of One Union, One Industry, MAWU merged with other metal unions in

Jabu often spoke at youth and women's rallies.

1987 to form a single national union, the National Union of Metalworkers of South Africa. The formation of this new giant strengthened the union's position.

As members of NUMSA, the women of Prestige were aware of what was happening to them. The union organised workshops and seminars and published pamphlets to educate its members. There was unity at Prestige. When May Day rallies, Women's Day rallies, education days and cultural events had to be organised, Prestige workers were always there. And the Prestige Choir could always be relied upon to sing at these events.

Jabu became known and respected through NUMSA, and through her courage in speaking out on public platforms at a time when it was very dangerous to do so.

While war brought terror and violence, it also brought secrets. Parents could no longer communicate with their children. As a friend of Jabu's says, "There is now no communication between parents and kids. This war has separated us from our families. The kids have got something bottled inside that we don't know. We are trying so hard to get involved in the struggle to find out what's happening to our kids, because all of a sudden they are so secretive. All of a sudden they come back home in the early hours of the morning, and you don't know whether your kid has been to kill somebody. And your kid will never say a word to you about killing, yet there is so much killing going on."

Jabu was very aware of the problems other parents were facing because of Linda's involvement in a defence team. She could see that Linda was no longer able to talk openly to Noma or his sisters. But he was able to speak to Jabu because they were both involved. Mamza was six years younger than Linda. She says she was quite close to him.

But from about 1985 she was suddenly shut out of his life. The time of secrets had begun.

It was confusing for Mamza, and frightening. "They used to talk politics, but they used to go to another room so we wouldn't hear anything, because many things were banned. When I grew up, I knew that I couldn't say anything about Mandela, because then the police would ask me, 'What do you know about Mandela?' Then maybe him or my mother would be in trouble."

The parents intervene

Because she listened to Linda and understood how his life was being disrupted as a result of the struggle, Jabu used to speak especially to the youth in her speeches. The youth came to love her and to seek her advice.

Nor was Jabu afraid of intervening in youth struggles. She was one of the parents who helped make peace when fighting broke out between the Azanian People's Organisation (AZAPO) and UDF youth. The parents called a meeting in Sobantu village, a friend recalls. "I remember the problem, where they were fighting. Jabu was one of the parents who said they could not fight each other and Inkatha at the same time. She contributed to their unity, because both organisations were of the oppressed."

Often, when friends used to visit the house, there were youth in the yard who had come to get advice from Jabu and to learn about the struggle. But the home was not very popular, because people were afraid of being exposed by going into Jabu's house, says one friend.

"Parents were keeping their children from going there

because they were afraid of Inkatha spies. But the children on their own wanted to go to her house because they were committed to the struggle."

"A great loss"

Noma also remembers the youth in the yard. "These young fellows, boys and girls, liked her very much. When I went to her place, especially in the afternoon, if she had not gone to the meeting, I would find them in the yard. Some sitting, some standing. I think they just liked to be there because she was like a mother to them.

"I think she had a good manner with them – even if they were doing something wrong she used to correct them. And they used to apologise. Some used to come for advice if they had problems.

"Even their mothers, these young people's mothers, used to bring their problems to Jabu's home. Even now, when I meet some of them, they say, 'Oh, it was a great loss to lose your sister, because we've got no one to help us with certain things now'."

Another comrade, who met Jabu through her work with detainees, explains how she would almost take over the role of parents: "She would phone up about youths who had been arrested and were in trouble and actually took over as a parent figure. Some of the other parents were opposed to what their children were doing, and would rather have them shipped off to another place to get on with their lives, to get on with their schooling.

"But as with Linda, the youths would perpetually want to come back to Pietermaritzburg because they felt they were needed here. In cases like that Jabu would often take over as the mother figure, trying to look after them."

At the last May Day rally at the Lay Centre – the last May Day rally Jabu was ever to speak at – she especially concentrated on the problems of the youth.

Her friends remember what she said: "She spoke about the conflict in Natal. Police attacking schools; police taking children from school to the jails. They were also shooting children in front of the teachers and children were fleeing for their lives. The advice Jabu gave was, 'Let us not give up. We must go to school even if we know that the education is poor.'

"Jabu said the women of Imbali should get organised, and be the backbone of the youth. She said she saw the youth being killed in the streets everywhere. The only way to save our kids was for the women to organise. She told us she was ready to die for what she said, because it was the truth."

ELEVEN

There is no peace

DURING THIS PERIOD JABU WAS interviewed about what was happening in Imbali. She took the opportunity to give a message to the women. This is what she said:

* * *

> We as mothers have a problem because we see the SAPs with the Inkatha people, and we see the Inkatha people carrying pistols without licences, and we know that they are being helped by the police.
>
> Sometimes, if there is an Inkatha funeral, the police come back into the townships, especially at Imbali, and they chase everyone. The Inkatha people also come inside the township and attack people, assaulting them with pistols.
>
> So we are being very much affected, especially at night. You can't sleep very well when right at midnight people are coming in. Someone is knocking at the front window,

the back door, the front door. After that you won't sleep at all. In the morning, your children are supposed to go to school and you are supposed to go to work. So there is no peace.

My message is to encourage women to struggle, even if they are not working, to be active within the community. They must help the community, especially the youth – help them when they have got problems.

The youth complain that their fathers are not helping, especially on the weekends they go off drinking. So the women must help the youth – they must call meetings and help them plan what to do.

※ ※ ※

TWELVE
Sisters of the Long March

THE "VIVA MOSS" CAMPAIGN and the Sarmcol campaign took Jabu overseas in 1988. The aim of the trip was to mobilise international support for the two campaigns. A colleague was chosen to accompany Jabu on the tour.

The two shop stewards were there to chaperone a group of five young girls from Mpophomeni. The girls were the daughters and sisters of the Sarmcol strikers. As part of the solidarity campaign, they had worked out a cultural event, *Sisters of the Long March*, which they were to perform in the UK.

The show, with singing and dancing, told of women's suffering as a result of the strike and the sacking of the workers. The two shop stewards wrote a part for themselves and performed in the show. "Our part was about problems we encountered as women in the workplace and in the community. We also worked with the youth, on their problems since their fathers went on strike. People were very happy with the show when it was finished."

Before they went overseas, the group spent many hours rehearsing and revising the show with Patti Henderson.[15] Patti remembers how dedicated the two shop stewards were, attending every rehearsal, no matter how exhausted they were.

Jabu's part was about the tragedy of young people's lives in the war. It told how young people could no longer stay at home and were hiding all over the township because Inkatha or the police were looking for them.

None of the group had ever been overseas before. Nor had they experienced the bitter cold of an English winter. They had difficulty getting out of bed in the morning; it was so cold.

Their schedule was tough. "We started at the Trade Union Council Centre in London. There we met the SACTU people, who welcomed us to their offices. After introductions, we sang some of our songs there for them, and told them our reasons for coming."

From there the tour began. The "Sisters" worked a 20-hour day, getting up at 7:00 am and working right through until 3:00 am. "There was a lot of work to be done. Sometimes we had to give two shows in the same

---

15 Update, October 2017: Patti Henderson was a cultural activist who, along with Ari Sitas and others, had been involved with the Junction Avenue Theatre Company in Johannesburg. Ari initiated the Culture and Working Life Project, which worked together with the COSATU Durban Workers' Cultural Local to develop plays with workers about their workplace struggles. Patti, together with Ari, Mi Hlatshwayo, Alfred Qabula and Debby Bonnin had worked on two plays with the Sarmcol workers that told about the workers' struggles. These plays were *The Long March* and *Bhambata's Children*. A third play, *Sisters of the Long March*, was about the struggles faced by the wives and daughters of the Sarmcol strikers. The history of these and other workers' plays is told in a book – *Organise and Act: The Natal Workers Theatre Movement 1983–1987* – written by Astrid von Kotze and published by the Culture and Working Life Project in 1988.

afternoon. And after that we had to discuss the issues. There were interviews – people from the radio, from the papers, from the TV.

"There were many questions – like, 'Now Jabu, you decided to come here, leave your husband and children. How did you manage to do that?' We said, 'Since we are shop stewards we are used to leaving our families behind'."

There were also visits to places of interest – including museums and castles. Of special interest to Jabu was a visit to the Greenham Common women. They were a group of women who camped out in the open on Greenham Common for over ten years to protest against the building of an American missile site nearby. The women lived in tents and shacks – "like *imijondolo*", says Jabu's colleague – in spite of the rain and snow. The "Sisters" performed for the Greenham Common women and told them about Mayekiso and the Sarmcol struggle.

"Jabu was very happy to be over there. She believed that people overseas were doing a lot of work for our struggle. She was also eager to go to America because we met someone there who made a videotape of us in Manchester. She said we should show the video to the women of America. Jabu was very eager to go there to share with those people, and to find out how their unions were working."

The "Sisters" came back happy and exhausted from their overseas tour. But there was to be no rest for them at home. The war was getting worse, as Jabu explained in a letter to her friends Chris and Lottie Bailie. Chris and Lottie work with the BRT Workers' Support Network in Cambridge.

* * *

P.O. Imbali 4503
South Africa

Hallo! Lottie and Chris

I am very glad as I am writing this letter to you. We had a pleasant journey on our way back. We arrived in Durban on Tuesday at 10:40 am. It was so hot. We had a problem – we didn't find anyone to pick us up to Pietermaritzburg. After two hours, we found someone waiting at a wrong exit at the airport. We were so upset as we had so many parcels.

We reached our families still doing well, though there is still a lot of unrest in this township. On 28.10.88 my brother-in-law's son was shot dead by anonymous men. He was going to get married in December. He was with his two brothers who escaped three shots in that same spot. He will be buried on 5.11.88. This unrest is getting worse really, and we do not know what to do.

We are missing England, people like yourselves … I remember your stories as I learned many things. If I had a phone I would phone you. Let's hope we shall meet again … Lottie, please remind Chris to post me those photos we took at Cambridge. I know Chris might be busy. I still thank you people as we had a pleasant time with you. But we hope to meet again if it happens.

Thank you,
Regards,
Jabu Ndlovu

* * *

Jabu won the hearts of many trade unionists the "Sisters" met on their travels. When she died, they held memorial services in places like London, Cambridge, Norwich and Liverpool. NUMSA and Jabu's family received many messages of support and solidarity from friends the "Sisters" made overseas.

THIRTEEN
Defending Stage I

As Jabu told Lottie and Chris, the war in Natal was getting worse. Since 1985, about 20 000 to 30 000 people had become refugees in Natal and thousands of homes had been burned. Many refugees were from Imbali, Edendale and Ashdown. But the violence had also spread to the townships around Durban, and to other places, like Sweetwaters, Mpumalanga, Hammarsdale and Mpophomeni. The death toll had long reached four figures.

Towards the end of 1988, as part of its peace campaign, COSATU decided to conduct research into the violence. Because of the many stories workers were bringing to the unions, the research concentrated on the role of the police.

The area COSATU chose to study was Imbali Stage I, because it seemed that most of the attacks were being carried out there. If you want to see how bad the violence was in Stage I, you just have to walk down Mthombothi Road, where Jabu and Jabulani once lived. Many houses bear the scars of the war. Some are completely destroyed. Others have smashed windows or doors, and walls blackened by fire. Many are deserted.

Warlords and gangs appeared to be operating with the support of the police. Police would arrive late at the scenes of attacks and they were often seen talking to warlords or vigilantes. They were sometimes seen driving around with Inkatha members, pointing out Comrades.

As a NUMSA member, and because of her work in the community, Jabu was asked to help with COSATU's research. The research led to a memorandum on the violence, which was published by COSATU early in 1989. The memorandum focused on the period from 20 November 1988 to 16 January 1989.

In March 1989, Jabu went with a group of lawyers and COSATU representatives to Johannesburg to tell the world about the violence in Imbali through a press conference. The memorandum named well-known Inkatha officials and warlords, who knew where Jabu lived and worked. It accused them of causing the violence. It accused the police of contributing to the violence.

Linda is arrested

The first case described in the memorandum is about Jabu's son, Linda. The report tells how Linda was arrested with a group of Comrades in November 1988 after a shooting and stoning incident involving an Inkatha official in Stage I. Evidence was that a prominent Inkatha member had fired shots at a Comrade, Skwababa Ngubane. Skwababa threw stones to chase his attackers away, and then fled.

About three hours later, another car arrived, this time

driven by the warlord's son. He was accompanied by a *kitskop* – a "special policeman". The *kitskop* shot at some youths, who threw stones and fired back. In the battle one of the youths, Mandla Zu Mthembu, was struck by a bullet in the hip.

About 15 minutes after the battle, two police vehicles drove up, with the Inkatha official and the warlord inside. They pointed out Linda and three other Comrades. Linda and the Comrades were arrested and charged with murder. There was no investigation into the shooting of Mandla Zu Mthembu.

It was the threat of this trial and the seriousness of the charge, which carried with it a possible jail sentence, that caused Linda finally to drop out of school. Previously, like hundreds of other youth living in the Pietermaritzburg area and in the townships around Durban, he had only been picked up now and then, held for a couple of days and then allowed to go free. The people of Imbali saw these random arrests as harassment, aimed at disrupting the lives of students and youth.

To get him away from the violence and the arrests, which were seriously disturbing his studies, Jabu had sent him to school in the country, at Msinga, in 1988. But he kept coming back to Imbali. And then, when he had what looked like a serious trial to face, he decided not to go back to school the following year.

This decision brought him into conflict with both his mother and his father, who were very worried by now. They believed that sending Linda away to school in the rural areas was the only way to save his life. But Linda remained determined. He felt he could not leave Imbali while his comrades and his community were under attack.

There were many family arguments about what to do.

Then in March 1989, a few months after the attack, Linda's case was dismissed. Linda and the three Comrades arrested with him went free.

The story about Linda is typical of many in the COSATU report. The memorandum includes 29 incidents of political violence recorded in about two months. It says that out of these, 16 were initiated by Inkatha members, three were initiated by Comrades, three were initiated by members of the South African Police, and seven were caused by unknown people.

In this violence, 15 people were killed and 14 wounded. There were 28 arrests; 26 of the people arrested were Comrades and only two were Inkatha members.

A commission of inquiry

Their research led COSATU to call for an independent commission of inquiry into the violence and police action in Pietermaritzburg. In spite of this call and others like it, no commission was ever set up.

Today, many people believe the attack on Jabu's home was connected to what was said in the COSATU memorandum. And when people talk about Jabu, they always remember that she was one of the people in the delegation to Johannesburg. They always remark on the courage of a Stage I resident who was prepared to speak out in defence of the people of Stage I.

FOURTEEN
The attack

Soon after her trip to Johannesburg, Jabu was off again. This time, she went as a delegate to the NUMSA congress in Johannesburg on May 20–21, representing Southern Natal. Harry Gwala, who lives at Dambuza, the next township down the Edendale Road from Imbali, was honoured at the congress.

Harry Gwala had been jailed in the 1960s and again in 1977 under the Terrorism Act. He had been released shortly before the NUMSA congress. The delegates elected him honorary president of NUMSA in recognition of his many years of commitment to the struggle and the trade union movement as an ANC and South African Communist Party member.

At the congress, Harry Gwala joined others in condemning the violence in Natal and speaking about peace initiatives.

The Natal violence was high on the congress agenda. The NUMSA president, Daniel Dube, said the trade union movement should do everything in its power to stop the violence in Natal. He told delegates: "If it means we should meet with Gatsha Buthelezi, we must do just that to ensure that the killings in Natal come to an end."

Resolutions on peace in Natal must have pleased Jabu. She also cheered when the union resolved to form stronger ties with community structures.

But because of the violence, the Natal delegates left early. They wanted to be home before dark.

Jabu and another delegate travelled in the same car. The driver dropped them off at Jabu's house at about five o'clock on Sunday, just as the sun was beginning to set. Tired after the long drive from Johannesburg, he said good-bye and went home.

That was the last time he ever spoke to Jabu. The other delegate drank a cup of tea, and she and Jabu discussed the congress. They were both exhausted, so Jabu's friend soon went home.

The friend went to bed early. Just after midnight, she was woken by the sound of shots coming from the direction of Mkhamba Road. "I thought they were attacking her because we had gone to the congress," she says. "I was very scared. I thought they were also coming for me. I ran to her house. When I got there, the girl, the daughter, had just died."

There were five people in the house. Jabulani and Jabu must have struggled to stop their attackers from coming in. But they failed.

Jabulani and Khumbu were killed in the attack. Khumbu died saving the life of her young sister, Luhle, by forcing her to run through the flames and out of the back of the house. Khumbu's body was found near the back door. She had apparently been shot as she emerged from the flames. Jabu, Luhle and Thabane, Jabu's nephew, were taken to hospital. Jabu had a bullet wound in the head and severe burns; Luhle and Thabane suffered burns on their legs.

"A sophisticated device"

According to witnesses, the house burned very fiercely. NUMSA said later this indicated that a sophisticated device was probably used to set it alight.

The house was so badly burned that at first, no one could find Jabulani's body. He was eventually found behind the door by people who came in the morning to pray for the family.

One of the first people on the scene that morning was the Anglican priest and community leader, Father Victor Afrikander, who came as soon as he heard what had happened. He led the prayers. (Twelve months later, Father Afrikander was also dead. He was shot while taking his granddaughter to school one morning. The story goes he was killed in revenge for the murder a few days earlier of the son of an Inkatha warlord. But it turned out that the warlord's son had been killed by a fellow *kitskonstabel*.)

Noma heard about the attack on Jabu's house on the Monday evening. "I didn't know then who was in the house, who was dead and who was not dead, till the following morning, because the people who were there didn't want to tell me.

"I was there the day before, the Sunday. I found Jabulani there and Linda. Jabulani was lying on the bed, reading his novel. Linda had just bathed and was dressing himself.

He said he was going out. It was about four o'clock in the afternoon. So he wasn't in the house because all the time he was being followed by the police."

Jabu's mother also heard late on Monday afternoon. Hours before the attack on Sunday, she had a feeling something terrible was going to happen. "The day before, I was not at home in the afternoon. I had attended a church meeting. At the church meeting I felt like rushing home, as if something bad was happening. When I came home, there was nothing. But it was as if something was going to happen – something had touched me like a sangoma.

"I went to sleep. On the Monday, a woman came and said she had received a phone call saying that they were injured. It was very painful. I was needed there urgently. My son, Temba, came to fetch me."

Jabu lived for ten days – long enough to name her killers before she died.

Gogo Mkhize was one of the first people to see Jabu in hospital. "When I came there, when I looked at her, I said, 'You are burned', and she said, 'Yes'. She was talking; she even laughed, saying, 'Mother, I will see you after being discharged'. I thought that she was going to get well."

Jabu asked her mother about the safety of her husband and daughter. Gogo Mkhize says she asked everyone who visited her about them. "I said he was okay, because I did not want to disturb her. I said Khumbu was okay, too. I said she was at Edendale Hospital. Jabu said I should bring them to her. I said I would."

A close friend and fellow worker visited her in hospital twice a day until she died. She was in the factory when she heard about the attack.

"The workers cried"

"The workers cried when they heard. People couldn't even eat. Like myself, I nearly died, because I could hardly even drink anything. It took me about a week to talk to other people. The first day I heard the news, I failed to work; I went back home.

"I visited her on the second day. Jabu and her daughter were in the same ward. After speaking to the daughter, I talked to Jabu. I said, 'Hallo, ma', as usual – I always called her ma – and she said, 'Hallo, my daughter'. I can actually hear the voice.

"She could not see because her eyes were swollen, you know. I said, 'How are you feeling?' She said, 'I am all right although I have pain from the burns'. She was very ill. I told her the workers were missing her, and that I was missing her.

"The following day she said to me, 'I know why I am in this condition now. But if I become well again I will go forward with the struggle. I am prepared, because there is no other way. I know what I was fighting for; I was fighting for my rights, and the rights for other people as well. I haven't done anything bad; that's why, if I get well again, I will go forward with the struggle.'

"That's where I saw this was a very strong woman. She was doing a lot of talking, asking about people, asking about the workers, saying I must give her regards to the workers.

"The only thing that hurt me was when she was asking for her husband," recalls the friend. "She said, 'Where's your dad? I'm worried about your dad and your sisters.' I said, 'Ma, dad is in hospital, and my sisters are all in hospital. As soon as they are well they will come and visit you.' I was hiding it from her because the nurses hadn't decided to let her be told the truth. They were afraid of her reaction.

"Jabu was very ill for a week. I remember the day when I last saw her. I heard that she was calling me for the whole night, and they phoned me at work. But they couldn't find me because I had attended the funeral of the husband and the daughter.

"When I came back to work, the management told me about the call. I went to the hospital. I said to her, 'Ma, you have been calling me.' She asked, 'What's the day today?' I said, 'It's Monday.' She asked me if I had any money because she wanted me to buy food for her children, and give them some pocket money. I said, 'Look here, there is no problem with that; just forget about it because the union is there.'

"The next day, I went again, and she said to me, 'Today I am not feeling well at all.' I left some cards from the workers and went away, because I could not stand to see her in that condition."

Jabu died two days later, of a lung infection resulting from the burns. She died not knowing that her husband and eldest daughter had been killed.

FIFTEEN
Calls for peace

AFTER JABU'S DEATH, COSATU and community organisations in Imbali called a three-day stayaway in Pietermaritzburg to protest against the violence and to mourn her death.

They also demanded an end to the killings and police misconduct. They demanded that warlords be jailed and called for the lifting of restrictions on funerals and ex-detainees. They called for an independent commission of inquiry into the role of the police. In response to the call, thousands of workers stayed away from their factories and workplaces on June 5, 6 and 7 to mourn for Jabu.

The violence that killed Jabu, Jabulani and Khumbu followed them to the grave. There is no communal cemetery in Impendle, so the tradition is that families bury their own dead near their houses. There are three graves in front of the Mkhize home, the last resting places of Phambano Mkhize and Jabu's brothers, Dumisani and Mzwandile. Gogo Mkhize wanted Jabulani and Khumbu to be buried

Jabu's body taken from St Mary's to the cemetery.

there, too.

The arrangements for the service at St Joseph's, where Jabu and Jabulani were married, had already been made. Workers had been notified and Jabu's friends and comrades from Prestige were preparing to travel to Impendle in spite of a police notice restricting the funeral.

The notice, issued only two days before the funeral, restricted the number of mourners to 200. It also banned flags, banners, pamphlets and the use of a public address system. It barred all speakers other than the minister, and forbade people from walking along the route.

Then, the day before the funeral, community councillors received anonymous threats: if the funeral took place at Impendle, they were told, the Natal violence would spread to their area.

"We heard someone had phoned the councillors, telling them they should not agree to have the funeral here. The person said they were going to come and burn the shops and houses. So the councillors refused permission," says a worker. "Somebody was also scaring Impendle people from going to the funeral in Pietermaritzburg. They said if they went, they shouldn't come back. People were willing to go, but they were scared. It was very confusing."

So Jabulani and Khumbu had to be buried in Mountain Rise cemetery in Pietermaritzburg, on May 29, two days before Jabu's death.

Jabu's funeral was scheduled to be held at Mountain Rise cemetery on Saturday, June 10. Suddenly, there was a banning order. The funeral could not be held. Police blamed the banning on the Pietermaritzburg Parks Department. They said the Parks Department did not permit "political" funerals to be held at weekends. The ban meant that workers would have difficulty attending the funeral.

The funeral was finally held on Monday, June 12. Shortly before it was due to begin, police issued a notice restricting it to 200 people. Armed police cordoned off St Mary's church – "like a guard of honour," says Thoko – and refused entry to all but 200 mourners. Among those left standing outside were members of Jabu's family, including Gogo Mkhize, Thoko and Bobo.

"They gave us five minutes to disperse"

"The police had a statement that they read to us, in English, Afrikaans and Zulu, saying we were not allowed in. The last one gave us five minutes to disperse. We left, because we did not know what was going to happen," says Thoko. "We went to the cemetery."

At Mountain Rise, things were no better. Hundreds of people were turned away. People left outside were told to sit in their cars. People moving from car to car were arrested. Those who did manage to get to the graveside were sjambokked by police as they left the cemetery. The 70-year-old ANC veteran, Harry Gwala, was among those who were hit.

One bus, full of mourners, was turned away at the cemetery gates. The driver was forced to return to Imbali via a freeway which took him through Slangspruit, a known warlord stronghold. When the passengers complained, they were told to disembark. Suddenly, vigilantes attacked and two people were stabbed.

At Prestige, the funeral led to the sacking of one of Jabu's friends. Management had told workers they could go to the funeral, but they would not be paid for the hours spent away from work. They would have to clock out if they wanted to go. Jabu's friend was fired because management believed she had told workers they did not have to clock out.

After the funeral, NUMSA issued a press statement condemning police action. "The police conduct is in marked contrast to their conduct at the recent funeral of a well-known Inkatha leader in Mpumalanga. It is reported that five to six thousand were allowed to attend that funeral. NUMSA once again repeats the call made by COSATU that an urgent independent Commission of Inquiry into police conduct in Pietermaritzburg is essential to restoring legality and peace in the area," the statement said.

The violence and the fact that members of her family could not be buried with their father made Gogo Mkhize very unhappy, says Thoko. "She couldn't understand. They were not the first ones to be killed in this war. Other people were taken from here and buried at their homes. We are the only unfortunate ones."

SIXTEEN
Linda

On 25 February 1990, a Sunday afternoon, Linda was shot dead in Imbali. This was the same day that the ANC leader, Nelson Mandela, came to Durban for the first time since his release after 27 years in prison. At the huge rally Durban people gave to welcome him, Mandela spoke about peace. He called on the Comrades to throw their weapons into the sea.

Linda had spoken about going to the rally, but in the end he did not go to Durban. It is not clear why he did not go. That evening, he was shot dead in a gun battle outside the house of an Inkatha warlord.

After his parents' death, Linda had gone into hiding in Durban. But he emerged from hiding in July 1989 to make a statement to the police about a shooting that had taken place the day before the attack on his home. As a result of the shooting, he was charged with possession of an illegal weapon.

At this trial, Linda pleaded not guilty. He told the court

that on Saturday, May 20, he had been watching some youths playing soccer in Stage I.

While he was sitting there, he saw two Imbali residents and Inkatha supporters, Mr and Mrs Mhlaluka, and a third person walking along Mthombo Road. As they approached Linda and his friends, Mr Mhlaluka reached for something, and Mrs Mhlaluka was searching in her bag.

Linda says he ran away immediately, believing they were attempting to draw firearms. While he was running, he says, he heard shots and shouting. He hid in the yard of a nearby house.

He then made his way home and told his father what had happened. Jabulani and Linda agreed it would be best if he did not sleep at home that night in case the house was attacked. So that Saturday he slept in one of the "safe houses" where he used to hide. He slept out again the following night, the Sunday, because he had heard of threats against his life.

His home was destroyed that night. On the Monday, May 22, a friend found Linda and told him about the attack. This was how he heard about the death of his father and sister.

Months later, at the trial at which he was accused of shooting at Mr and Mrs Mhlaluka, Linda was found not guilty. Evidence at the trial was that Mrs Mhlaluka had been injured in the shooting. Although Linda was acquitted, the trial fuelled rumours that he was the target when his parents' home was attacked. People still say it was Linda the attackers were after.

On the run for three years

After the trial, in spite of threats to his life, Linda felt he could not stay away from Imbali and leave others to defend the community. So he kept going back there.

Linda never really explained why he had to go back. Some people say he wanted to avenge the attack on his family. Others say he just needed to be with his friends and the people he loved.

By the time of his death, Linda had been in hiding – living on the run from the police and the warlords – for over three years. He told Mamza about his anger about always having to hide. "He used to say, 'We don't have any freedom. We can't go out because of these people.' He couldn't even see his friends; he couldn't do things that he wanted to."

Years of hiding had made having a home very important to Linda. Some months after Jabu's death, he started speaking about repairing the house at Number 437 Mkhamba Street so that he could live there with his sisters and brothers. Shortly before he was shot, he asked the Comrades to clean up the garden and was planning to repair the roof and paint the walls.

Before 1985, Mamza remembers, Linda used to play with her and Luhle. "I was still very young. The thing that I know was that I was always very happy to see him as one of the best people. I remember he was a Cub at school and he was the best one. My parents used to encourage him so much that I also decided to be a Girl Guide because of him."

Like his mother, Linda was respected as an advisor: "I always remember him saying you must listen to other people's ideas; you mustn't just ignore other people's ideas. When they had meetings he used to advise them where to meet. He used to tell people, you must know what you are. Like some people would say, 'No, I'm not an Inkatha member, I'm not a UDF member', or something. Well, he used to tell them, 'You must know what you are, because it's no use saying you don't know, because when Inkatha people meet you, and you say you don't know, they will say you are scared, you don't want to tell them. And when UDF people meet you, they will say you are scared and don't want to tell them. So it's better that you know yourself where you are.'"

Linda's life wasn't all serious. "If it was time for fun, he would have fun as long as we were all having fun," says Mamza. But if it was time for seriousness, then he'd be serious.

"He used to like music – he liked Mzwakhe Mbuli very much, and then Stimela and Mango Groove he used to like, and Amampondo – and wait, I want to tell you this – he used to like the OJs very much. And Marvin Gaye.

"He liked reading, he liked making his own things, like making cards. He used to like dancing. He was a good *Pantsula* dancer. I remember he won a set of cooking pots at a competition at the hall because he danced very well.

"He also liked soccer, but then he stopped liking soccer when he got involved in politics. Then he used to like cultural things, like going to poetry workshops."

"Most of his friends had died"

"He was a very funny person. He used to like imitating people on TV and to make fun of them. And maybe when he was missing one of his friends he would do whatever the friend did, you know, just to make people laugh," says Mamza.

She remembers how two deaths in particular, in the middle of 1989, made Linda very angry. "I remember when we started staying here, just after our home was burned, two of his best friends were killed, Gandaya Biyase and Mandla Zu Mthembu. But they were killed on the same day. I think he was mad at that because Gandaya was still a young chap, and these big people attacked him. It made no sense.

"Most of his friends had died; it really affected him. Sometimes he would just sit. To me he never looked happy, but I know he tried, because he didn't want us to know that he was so unhappy."

About a week after his death, Linda was buried at Mountain Rise cemetery. At the funeral, members of the Imbali Youth Organisation bent down and kissed him as he lay in his coffin.

"I think it was because no one really expected Linda's death," says Mamza. "Maybe they just wanted to touch him for the last time. When I did it ... I don't know. He had a bandage on. I saw he had a wound on his head, and I just wanted to touch him."

SEVENTEEN
Warlords stand trial

ON 28 AUGUST 1989, three people were charged with the murders of Jabu, Jabulani and Khumbu. They were Thulani Ngcobo, Petros Ngcobo and Frederick Mhlaluka, all from Imbali.

Thulani Ngcobo told the court he knew nothing about the incident and was innocent. He said on the day in question he had been at home asleep. He was also questioned about the deaths of 11 other people, and denied knowledge of these killings, too. The three men were refused bail, and the trial was postponed.

In a separate court hearing, Jerome Mncwabe, a well-known Inkatha warlord and community councillor in Imbali, was also charged with the three murders. He was granted bail of R750, and the trial was postponed.

Over the next few months, there were two events which affected the trials.

The first was the shooting by gangsters of Petros Ngcobo's brother, Michael Thu Ngcobo. Michael was the person accused of harassing Jabu after the Moses Mayekiso protests at Prestige. He was killed outside a tearoom in Pietermaritzburg on New Year's Day, 1990.

The second was the shooting of one of the accused, Jerome Mncwabe. He was killed about two weeks after Father Victor Afrikander in May 1990. Rumours were that he was killed to avenge Father Afrikander's murder.

Michael Thu Ngcobo's killing led to the acquittal of his brother, Petros. At his trial in August 1990, Petros Ngcobo was charged with ten murders – including those of the Ndlovu family – seven attempted murders and four charges of arson.

The state led evidence that Petros Ngcobo's gun had been used in the killings and that bullets found at the scenes of the attacks were fired from his gun. Petros Ngcobo told the court that he knew nothing about the attacks. He said he often lent his gun to his brother, Michael Thu.

The judge accepted that there were grounds to believe that Petros Ngcobo had lent his gun to others. He said the court could not prove beyond reasonable doubt that Petros knew what his brother might use the gun for. There was also insufficient evidence to link Ngcobo conclusively to any of the attacks. So Petros Ngcobo was acquitted.

The trials of Thulani Ngcobo and Frederick Mhlaluka are not yet over. The two men are still in custody, awaiting trial.[16]

---

16 Update, October 2017: No one was ever convicted for the killings. This matter went before the Truth and Reconciliation Commission. Their final report had this to say:

"In August 1989, Thulani Ngcobo, Mr Petros Ngcobo and Mr Fredrick Mhlaluka, all of Imbali, were charged with the killings of Jabu, Jabulani and Khumbu Ndlovu. They were denied bail. In a separate hearing, Jerome Mncwabe was also charged with the three murders. He was granted bail of R750. Mncwabe was killed in May 1990. Michael Thu Ngcobo was killed on

1 January 1990. His killing led to the acquittal of his brother, Petros, who told the court in August 1990 that Michael Thu had often borrowed his gun, which had been ballistically linked to the killings of the Ndlovus. Petros Ngcobo told the court that he knew nothing of the attack on the Ndlovus and others for which he was charged. The judge accepted this evidence and Ngcobo was acquitted. No further convictions have followed." [Source: http://sabctrc.saha.org.za/reports/volume3/chapter3/subsection33.htm]

EIGHTEEN
Conclusion: The trust

TODAY, JABU'S CHILDREN ARE SCATTERED. They are at schools in different parts of the country. Their aunt, Noma, says they have remained strong in spite of what has happened to them. They are determined to finish school.

During school holidays Bobo, Mamza and Luhle sometimes stay together when there is a safe house for them. If it is possible, they visit Gogo Mkhize and Sanele in Impendle. The four children are happy when they can be together, because then they can speak about Jabu and Jabulani. They also remember Khumbu and Linda. "Luhle especially suffers about Linda, because they had that close relationship," says Mamza.

The children hardly ever return to Imbali Stage I, although they miss their old friends and schoolmates. The family believe it is safer for them to avoid Stage I, at least until the trial is over.

NUMSA, the family and Jabu's friends and Comrades have helped and supported the children, but their future remains uncertain. Like thousands of other children made orphans by the violence, they face major financial difficulties. It is for this reason that NUMSA decided to set up a Trust Fund in Jabu's name. The Trust is to provide for the education of children whose families have lost breadwinners because of the war.

The idea was inspired by Jabu's generosity. When people speak about Jabu, they remember her skills as an organiser, especially of women. They remember her support for the youth. They remember her courage. But they also remember her willingness to share.

As Mamza put it, "We were not a rich family, though we were not poor as well. But she used to give in such a way that we also accepted it. She used to give what little she had, and we didn't moan about it. We didn't say that we also don't have clothes and so on, because we seemed to understand what she was doing. She used to like people a lot. She used to take care of any person in need."

In setting up the Trust, the union said, "There are many other children who have been deprived and who now live on the streets. This will not happen to Jabu's children because she was an important and well-known leader, and the union will see to it that they are taken care of. Jabu would have expected this support from us. But she would also have asked, what about the other children who have faced this problem?"

We have written this book to raise funds for the Trust. All profit from its sale will go towards the future of Jabu's children and the children of the many others who have died.

We have also told Jabu's story to show the suffering and courage of communities ravaged by the war, and especially to tell the stories of the women. Jabu never accepted that a woman's place was in the home and in the kitchen. She fought not only for workers' rights and justice, but also for women's emancipation.

Thousands of women have struggled to keep their families together in the war; many have fought and died. We only know the names of some of them. Jabu's story is a tribute to the courage of all of these women.

Women whose names are known, killed in political violence in the Natal Midlands, 1987 to 1990

1987

Linda Zwane (19)
Thembi Zondi (20)
Buyi Xulu (21)
Thuli
Zandile Sangweni
Beauty Mthethwa
Nkosikazi Cele
Fikile Ndlovu
Lindiwe Ngubane
Angelina Maqhikila Mkhize
Petronnela Zandile Mkhize
Anna Mathonsi
Tebu Majola (19)
Polly Mkhize (18)
Nkosikazi Nxumalo
Elise Thabethe (37)
Mayandise Thabethe (46)
Maria Mhlongo

1988

Nkosikazi Khumalo
Busisiwe Buthelezi

Nkosikazi Hadebe
Silindile Cele (19)
Nkosikazi Dladla
Christina Khumalo
Florence Kunene (39)
Delisile Kunene (8)
Zamaswazi Kunene (6)
Flora Ndlela (60)
Thembani Phillippina Nkomo (67)
Ester Molevu (61)
Nkosikazi Magwaza
Thathani Madondo (37)
Phumzile Sholoni Kunene (29)
Gabi Masilo (27)
Nonsikelelo Rejoice Mabaso (16)
Nkosikazi Khumalo
Nkosikazi Ndlovu
Lilian Bonakele Zondi (51)
Mabel Zuma
Vera Mdunge
Gertrude Mhlongo (70)
Nkosikazi Dlamini
Patience Ndlovu (14)
Zetho Shangase (29)
Dudu Shangase (36)
MaHadebe Ntuli (40)
Sikile Zondi (25)
Marietha Xaba (45)
Sara Nyoka (66)
Sdedewu Sithole (60)
Nkosazane Nkehli
Nkosikazi Nkehli

Rebecca Namane Ndlovu (13) (missing)
Thandi Nompumelelo Kheswa (10) (missing)
Xolisile Ndlovu (15)
Sibongile Zondi
Gretta Dlamini

1989

Philile Dlamini (early 20s)
Lina Lolo Moloi
Thokozile 'Khopho Masuku (22)
Nkosikazi Mlotshwa
Silindile
Delisile Khumalo (12)
Zodwa Khumalo (25)
Pretty Nomthandazo Mnikathi (17)
Babazile Florah Kheswa (67)
Fikile Florence Malunga (31)
Melta Makhoba (30)
Ntombifikile Elsie Ngxongo (50)
Bongi Dladla
Mita Ndonkweni (60)
Alvinah Nkosi (48)
Khumbuzile Ndlovu (22)
Jabulisile Florence Ndlovu (41)
Nsangiwe Shoba
Norah Mndaweni (25)
Margaret Ndlovu (52)
Nkosikazi Chonco (58)
Metta Zondi (56)
Roselina Nomusa Nsizwana (17)

Busisiwe Buthelezi
Philomena Makhaye
Ntokozo Ngcobo (16)
Lindiwe Shange (2)
Philliphina Duduzile Dlamini (50)
Maureen Nokuthula Dlamini (20)
Nqobile Zuma (2)
Duduzile Ntinga (27)

1990

Idah Mbanjwa (42)
Thokozile Eslina Mbanjwa (21)
Makhosazane Vilakazi (25)
Nofo Nzimande (35)
Nkosikazi Ngcobo
Catherine Mkhize
Nkosazane Mkhize
Mighty Mkhize
Khosi Vilakazi
Phindile Mtolo (4)
Josephina Dlamini (50)
Hlehle Carol Zondi (21)
Thembi
Sylvia Fikile Shabalala
Phumelele Shabalala
Zodwa Msomi (22)
Beauty Gwala
Busisiwe Zondi
Noma Zondi (1)
Nelisiwe Ngubane (17)

Nkosikazi Ngcobo
Thokoza Jeanette Basi (14)
Nomthandazo Precious Basi (15)
Lindeni Bhengu
Nomusa Rosemary Dlamini (15)
Pauline Dlamini (50)
Ruth Dudu Hlongwana
Flora Khonzeni Khumalo
Thulisile Langa (31)
Khethiwe Madlala (35)
Lilian Magubane (48)
Joyce Mazibuko (43)
Thobile Matutu Mbanjwa (19)
M. Mjodala
Nomfundo Mkhize (7)
Ntombifuthi Grace Mkhize
Emerentia Pheri Mncwabe (39)
Selestine Mncwabe (27)
Rose Mtolo (75)
Nobuhle Ndlovu (17)
Margaret Thandiwe Ndlovu (12)
Dominica Ngcobo (38)
Matezi Ngcobo (41)
Khokhiwe Ngubane
Josephinah Ngubane (60)
Jabu Ngubane
Elizabeth Ntuli (50)
Dololo Nzama (42)
Agnes Shalazile Shezi (30)
Benedicta Shibe (28)
Mantanti Agnes Sibisi (60)
Getrude Skhosana

Emerentia Marjorie Taderera
Paulina Thusi (58)
Grace Cabangani Zondi
Qondi Florence Zondi
Grace Zuma

Index

Numbers in italics indicate photos.

African National Congress (ANC), 20, 53, 71
Afrikander, Father Victor, 123, 138
agriculture
    commercial, 4, 10, 11, 12
    subsistence, 16
    See also labour tenancy
Alcan Aluminium, 18, 19
Alex Carriers, 19
amakhosi, 5, 8
Azanian People's Organisation (AZAPO), 107

Bantu Labour Act (1964), 72
Battle of Ncome, 3
Beaumont Commission, 60
betterment planning, 12, 13, 14
Bhambatha kaMancinza, 8
Bhambatha Rebellion, 9
Bhambatha's Children, 113n15
Biyase, Gandaya, 136
black spots, 11–12, 13
    See also forced removals
Bolton, Harriet, 18
Bonnin, Debby, 113n15
border industries, 15, 17, 23n10
BTR Sarmcol, 9, 18
    strike (1985), 24, 25, 26, 94, 95–9, 112
Buthelezi, Mangosuthu (Gatsha), 27n11, 27n12, 29, 90, 91, 122

Caprivi trainees, 27
Chemical Workers Industrial Union (CWIU), 19
civil war, 2, 25–30, 35, 89–94, 106–7, 117–20
    See also: violence
Clairvoux Mission, 48
colonialism, 2, 3–10, 30
Colony of Natal, 4, 5, 8, 10, 15
Complaints Adjudication Board, 28
Comrade Moss, *See* Mayekiso, Moses
Conac Engineering, 20
Congress of South African Students (COSAS), 28, 90
Congress of South African Trade Unions (COSATU), 21n9, 90
    cultural work, 113n15
    impact of violence, 25, 28–30, 117–18

"Report on Natal Violence"
(1989), 29–30, 117–18
Crown lands, 6
Culture and Working Life Project,
113n15
Cunningham-Brown, Jeannette, 20
customary law, 6

decentralisation (industrial), 13
deproclamation, 12, 13
Development Trust and Land Act
(1936), 12n7
Dick Whittington Shoes, 23
Dingane, 3
Duma, Robert, 93
Durban Strikes (1973), 18, 71, 72

Federation of South African Trade
Unions (FOSATU), 20, 22, 25
Ferallroys, 23
Food and Allied Workers Union
(FAWU), 101
forced removals, 12, 16
See also black spots

General Factory Workers' Benefit
Fund (GFWBF), 18
Gomane, 44, 45, 49, 52
Greenham Common, 114
group areas, 12
Group Areas Act (1950), 16, 56
Gwala, Harry, 18, 121, 130

Henderson, Patti, 113n15
Hidden Voices Project, ix
Hlatshwayo, Mi, 113n15
homestead economy, 4, 9

Imbali, 17, 35, 36, 55–6
Imbali Civic Association (ICA), 90,
93–94
Imbali Community Council, 90
Imbali Youth Organisation (IYO),
28, 90, 91–4, 104, 136
Impendle, 7, 10, 14, 17, 43, 55, 95
industrialisation, 10, 15–25
Industrial Council, 21
influx control, 14, 17

Inkatha Freedom Party (IFP), 24,
25–30, 35–6, 94
Inkatha Youth Brigade, 97
Sarmcol strike, 96
vigilantes, 25

Junction Avenue Theatre Company,
113n15

kitskonstabels, 27, 28, 102, 104, 123
Khumalo, MZ, 27n11
Koornhof, Piet, 91–2
KwaMakhutha massacre, 27n11

labour tenancy, 6, 11, 12–13, 42
land
  dispossession of, 2, 7–8, 10–14,
  16
  ownership patterns, 3n2
  tenure by Africans, 7
Land Act (1913), 10
Langalibalele, 8
legislation, racial, 2, 8, 11, 14
liaison committees, 19, 20, 71, 72
Long March, The, 96, 97, 113n15
Luthuli, Duluxolo, 27n11

Mabaso, Joseph, 97
Makhathini, John, 21, 71, 74, 75, 82
Mayekiso, Moses (Comrade Moss),
24, 97–9
Mbanjwa, Moses, 19–20
Metal and Allied Workers Union
(MAWU), 19, 20, 21, 22, 65, 66
  and COSATU, 90
  formation, 72
  at Prestige, 69–71, 74–7, 79–81
  Sarmcol strike, 95–7
  violence, 94
  women's issues, 85–6, 87
Mhlaluka, Frederick, 133, 137–9
migrant labour, 9, 10–14
Mission Reserves Act (1903), 7
Mkhize, Bongi, 59, 61
Mkhize, Dumisani, 46, 53
Mkhize, Ina Zuma (Gogo), 10–11,
41–2, *44*, 47–8
  attack and funerals, 124, 130, 131

grandchildren, 52, 53–4, 60, 65, 140
and Jabulani, 60–1, 127
Mkhize, Mzwandile, 53
Mkhize, Noma, 41, 45–8, 60, 61, 66, 101, 102
Mkhize, Phambano Petrus (1911–1976), 9, 10–11, 42–7, 53, 127
Mkhize, Thoko, 45–8, 130
Mncwabe, Jerome, 137, 138
Mnikathi, Filomena, 96
Mpophomeni, 25, 95, 96
Mthembu, Mandla Zu, 119, 136
Mxenge, Victoria, 25

Natal Agricultural Union, 11
Natal Code of Native Law, 6
Natal Native Trust, 5
Natal Worker History Project, x
National Union of Metalworkers of South Africa (NUMSA), x, 21–2, 37, 65
   formation of, 104–6
   Jabu's funeral, 131
   Women's Forum, 24
National Union of Textile Workers (NUTW), 19, 20
Natives (Abolition of Passes) and Co-ordination of Documents Act (1952), 11
Natives Land Commission (1916), 10
Native Trust and Land Act (1936), 10
   Amendment of (1956), 11
Ndlovu, Bobo, 57, 60, 64, 65, 67, 101, 102, 130, 140
Ndlovu, Jabulani (1947–1989), 14, 51, 100
   death and funeral, 29, 36, 122–3, 129
   marriage and home life, 52–3, 63–6
   sports, 61
   view of the unions, 23
   working life, 52, 60
Ndlovu, Jabulile Florence (1947–1989), 14, *50*, *105*
   birth and childhood, 45–7
   death and funeral, 122–6, 129–31
   death threats, 97–8, 100, 103
   education, 47–51, 59
   marriage and home life, 52–3, 63–7
   MAWU, 72–3, 74, 78–81, 82–8
   role of women, 110–11
   working at Prestige, 21–2, 57
   working with youth, 107–9
   working women, 59–60
Ndlovu, Khumbu (1965–1989), 51, 52, 53, 60, 61, 65, 66, 101
   death and funeral, 29, 122–3, 127, 129
Ndlovu, Linda (1968–1990), 53, 60, 61–2, 65, 66–7
   arrest, 118–20
   and the Comrades, 36, 103
   and COSAS, 28
   death, 133
   effect of violence, 29, 100
   and the IYO, 92–3
   on the run, 132–6
   threats against, 101–3
Ndlovu, Luhle (1977–), 60, *64*, 65, 67, 101, 140
   fire-bombing, 30, 122–3
Ndlovu, Mamza, 57, 60, *64*, 65, 101, 102, 106–7, 140
Ndlovu, Moses, 20–21
Ndlovu, Sanele (1980–), 54, 61, *64*, 65, 140
Ndlovu, Thabane, 30, 123
Ngcobo, Michael Thu, 98, 137–8
Ngcobo, Petros, 137
Ngcobo, Thulani, 137, 138
Ngubane, Simon, 96–7
Ngubane, Skwababa, 118
Ngwenya, Skhumbuzo, 91
Nhlabamkhosi, 9, 41, 42, 45
Ntombela, Muzi, 91
Nxamalala, 9
Nxamalala Secondary School, 49–50

Pietermaritzburg
   1973 Strikes, 19

industrialisation of, 10, 15, 23
  violence in, 26–7, 28
poll taxes, 8
Port Natal, 3
Prestige Choir, 23, 87–8, 106
Prestige Kitchenware, 17, 21, 22, 57, 58
  Jabu's funeral, 130–1
  MAWU, 71, 74–7
  working conditions, 59, 69–71, 78–9
proletarianisation, 2

Qabula, Alfred, 113n15

recession (1980s), 23
Regional Decentralisation Strategy, 23n10
relocations, 11–12, 16
Republic of Natalia, 3
reserves, 4, 5, 8, 10, 12n6
responsible government, 10

Sarmcol, *See* BTR Sarmcol
Sarmcol Workers Health Committee, 96
Schreiner, Geoff, 21, 71, 74, 76–7
Scottish Cables, 18, 19, 22
Shaka, 3
Shepstone, Theophilus, 4, 5
Shepstone System, 5, 6
  See also reserves
shop stewards
  committees, 20
  role of, 21, 22, 82
  Shop Stewards Councils, 22, 24, 25
  women as, 85–6
Sibiya, Micca, 97
Sibiya, Phineas, 25, 79, 96
Sisters of the Long March, 24, 112–16
Sitas, Ari, 113n15
Slangspruit, 58
South African Congress of Trade Unions (SACTU), 17, 72
South African Native Trust (SANT), 5, 11

State Security Council, 27n11

Tomlinson Commission (1955), 15n8
Trade Union Advisory and Co-ordinating Council (TUACC), 19
trade unions
  divisions in, 30
  independent trade union movement, 2, 15, 17–18
  recognition agreements, 22
Transport and General Workers Union (TGWU), 19

Union of South Africa, 10
United Democratic Front (UDF), 25–30, 35–6
  formation of, 89
  UDF Youth, 107

United Workers Union of South Africa (UWUSA), 90–1, 96
urbanisation, 15–25

violence, 2, 26, 31, 121–2
  impact on COSATU, 28–9, 117–18
  vigilantes, 25, 36
  and women, 28
  See also civil war
Viva Moss campaign, 98, 112
Volksraad, 3
Von Kotze, Astrid, 113n15
Voortrekker Republic, 3

wage labour, 4, 5, 6–7, 10
Wages Board, 17
Wages Commission, 17–18
Weenen, 13
white supremacy, 8
women, subjugation of, 6

Zondi, Lawrence, 9
Zondi people, 8, 9, 9n5
Zuma, Mconjwana (Chief) 9, 11, 13, 45, 53